Poor Folk

*A Heartfelt Story of Love, Poverty,
and Human Struggle*

A Modern Translation

Adapted for the Contemporary Reader

Fyodor Dostoevsky

Table of Contents

Preface - Message to the Reader

Rebuilding the Greatest Library in Human History

Thousands of years ago, the Library of Alexandria was the heart of global knowledge — a sanctuary where the wisdom of every known civilization was gathered and shared freely.

And then, it was lost.

Now, we're rebuilding it — and you are invited to join us.

At the Library of Alexandria, we've set out to make every book available to *every person on Earth* — not just in print, but in every language, every format, and for every reader.

Here's how we do it:

- **Deluxe Print Editions at True Printing Cost** - Order any book as a high-quality paperback, elegant hardcover, or stunning boxset — and only pay what it costs to print. No markups. No middlemen.
- **Unlimited Access to the Greatest Works** - Enjoy thousands of timeless classics — from Plato to Shakespeare to Tolstoy — in beautiful, modern eBook and audiobook editions. Read and listen without limits — for every reader, everywhere.
- **Modern Translations for Every Language & Dialect** - We're reimagining the classics in clear, accessible language — and translating them into every dialect imaginable. Everyone deserves to understand humanity's greatest ideas.

When you visit **LibraryofAlexandria.com**, you're not just accessing books — you're joining a global movement to restore, preserve, and share the wisdom of civilization.

Join us today at LibraryofAlexandria.com

Together, we'll ensure the light of human wisdom never fades again.

With gratitude,
The Modern Library of Alexandria Team

Visit:

www.libraryofalexandria.com

Or scan the code below:

Introduction

The Dawn of Dostoevsky:
A Tender Portrait of Poverty, Dignity, and Human Connection

Poor Folk (Russian: Bednye Lyudi), first published in 1846, marked the astonishing literary debut of a 24-year-old Fyodor Dostoevsky, instantly propelling him into the center of the Russian literary world. Hailed by some contemporaries as the next Gogol, Dostoevsky became an overnight sensation not with a sweeping epic or a daring philosophical treatise, but with this quiet, intimate, epistolary novel. Told entirely through a series of letters between two impoverished residents of St. Petersburg—Makar Devushkin, an aging government copyist, and Varvara Dobroselova, a young woman from a fallen aristocratic family—Poor Folk is a poignant, humane, and deeply emotional exploration of poverty, pride, love, and human dignity.

Though modest in scope, Poor Folk is monumental in its moral vision. It is not a political novel, but it is deeply political in its insistence that the poor are not caricatures, but full human beings with complex emotions, inner lives, and moral depth. It is not a love story in the traditional sense, but it is suffused with tenderness, longing, and the aching beauty of affection denied fulfillment. It is not a revolutionary work, yet it quietly challenges the indifference of a society that reduces people to their economic status.

Written in the wake of the industrialization and bureaucratization of 19th-century Russia, Poor Folk gives voice to those who had little voice in the grand narratives of history. It does not idealize the poor, nor does it demonize the wealthy. Instead, it dwells on the space in

3

between—on the quiet tragedies, daily humiliations, and small victories of ordinary people trying to live with dignity in a world that often overlooks them.

This modern translation presents Poor Folk in clear, accessible language, preserving the gentle irony, subtle emotional shifts, and quiet lyrical quality of Dostoevsky's original. The aim is not to modernize its themes—for they are already timeless—but to make its characters speak to the contemporary reader as vividly and humanly as they did to Dostoevsky's first audience.

To read Poor Folk today is to be reminded of the enduring human truths Dostoevsky would later explore more dramatically: the need to be seen, the dignity of suffering, the tragedy of unmet love, and the spiritual cost of poverty. It is also to witness the birth of one of literature's most compassionate and searching voices—one that would go on to write some of the greatest novels ever conceived, but which here, in its first utterance, is already unmistakably and brilliantly Dostoevsky.

A Portrait in Letters: Structure, Style, and the Emotional Terrain of Poverty

One of the most distinctive features of Poor Folk is its epistolary format. The novel is composed entirely of letters exchanged between Makar Devushkin and Varvara Dobroselova, creating a dual narrative that offers deep insight into both characters' inner lives while maintaining a sense of immediacy, intimacy, and emotional vulnerability. This form is not merely a stylistic choice; it is essential to the novel's moral and emotional impact.

By using letters, Dostoevsky allows readers to witness the private thoughts, hesitations, and yearnings of two people who have little else to cling to besides each other. The letter format creates a dialogue that is both deeply personal and tragically one-sided—each writer pours out their soul, but their words can never fully bridge the gulf of class, shame, or circumstance that keeps them apart. It is through these letters that we see how love, concern, resentment, jealousy, and sacrifice interweave and evolve, all under the shadow of economic insecurity.

Makar Devushkin is one of Dostoevsky's earliest and most moving character studies. A meek, aging clerk, he lives in humiliating poverty in a boarding house, subsisting on a meager salary and enduring the daily slights of society. Yet he clings fiercely to his pride. He buys clothes he cannot afford, copies documents with obsessive care, and defends the honor of his class and his beloved Varvara with trembling dignity. His love for Varvara is paternal, romantic, and devotional all at once—a complicated mixture of self-sacrifice and longing that is never fully requited but never dies.

Varvara, for her part, is a young woman who has fallen from gentility into hardship. Her letters reveal a delicate sensibility, a capacity for empathy, and a growing sense of fatalism. She appreciates Makar's love but cannot return it in kind. Her decision to marry a wealthier suitor by the end of the novel is not cold-hearted—it is a tragic capitulation to the realities of a world where love alone is not enough. Through her, Dostoevsky explores the limits of self-sacrifice and the cruel choices poverty imposes on women.

The brilliance of the novel lies in its tone. There is no melodrama, no grand gesture. The pain is quiet, persistent, and cumulative. We feel the weight of every missed meal, every embarrassing outfit, every condescending glance. We see how poverty is not just a lack of money but a slow erosion of self-worth. And yet, through it all, there is beauty. There is humor. There is love. And there is an unbreakable humanity that refuses to be extinguished.

Dostoevsky also weaves in subtle literary commentary. Throughout the letters, Makar discusses his reading habits, often comparing his own experiences to those in the popular fiction of the day. These meta-literary references serve both as a defense of the "low" lives Dostoevsky is portraying and as a critique of the sentimental literature that ignores the harsh truths of poverty. In doing so, Dostoevsky positions Poor Folk as both a work of fiction and a challenge to fiction—to write not about ideals, but about people.

Dignity and Despair:
The Spiritual and Social Vision of Dostoevsky's
First Novel

While Poor Folk lacks the theological depth and philosophical range of Dostoevsky's later masterpieces, it already contains the moral compass and spiritual vision that would define his work. At its core, this is a novel about human dignity in the face of social invisibility. It is a protest—not against a particular regime or policy—but against the soul-crushing effect of being unseen, unheard, and unloved.

For Dostoevsky, poverty is not simply an economic condition—it is a spiritual ordeal. Makar and Varvara do not suffer only from hunger or cold. They suffer from shame. From isolation. From the fear that they do not matter. And in this suffering, Dostoevsky discovers his central theme: that every human being, no matter how poor, weak, or broken, contains a spark of infinite value.

This spiritual humanism is what sets Dostoevsky apart from both the realists and the romantics of his time. He is not interested in portraying poverty as noble or picturesque. Nor is he content to present it as a social problem to be fixed from the outside. He wants to show what it feels like from the inside—to make the reader inhabit the daily degradation, the silent prayers, and the desperate clinging to small joys that define life on the margins.

And yet, he also shows how this degradation is not the final word. Makar, for all his weaknesses, loves with extraordinary devotion. Varvara, though worn down by circumstance, retains her gentleness and intelligence. Even as the world turns its back on them, they reach out to each other. They write. They hope. They endure.

This moral endurance is the first flowering of Dostoevsky's lifelong concern with the redemptive power of love, humility, and suffering. It is here, in Poor Folk, that we see the embryonic form of his later heroes—those who suffer silently, who are mocked by society, who are often ridiculous but whose souls shine with unexpected light. Makar Devushkin is the spiritual ancestor of Prince Myshkin, of Alyosha Karamazov, of Sonia Marmeladova. He is not strong or noble or wise. But he is kind. And in Dostoevsky's moral universe, that is the greatest strength of all.

The novel also quietly explores gender and power. Varvara's fate is a reminder of how women, especially those without wealth or family, were often forced to choose between survival and self-respect. Her eventual marriage is not a betrayal of Makar, but a desperate attempt to escape destitution. Dostoevsky does not judge her. He mourns her loss—and the loss of a world in which love might have triumphed over money.

Poor Folk is a short novel, but its emotional and ethical scope is vast. It is a story of two people who try, in the midst of hardship, to preserve their sense of self. It is a letter to the forgotten. And it is a challenge to every reader: to see the invisible, to love the unlovable, and to believe that even the poorest life contains something sacred.

In this modern translation, the goal is not simply to update the language, but to preserve the soul of the book. Dostoevsky's Russian is sometimes ornate, sometimes plain, but always sincere. His characters speak with the awkwardness, passion, and quiet dignity of real people. Our aim is to let those voices ring true—to let Makar and Varvara speak not as artifacts of the past, but as living souls whose struggles still echo in our world today.

As you begin Poor Folk, you are entering not just a story, but a conversation—a correspondence of hearts that will move you, challenge you, and perhaps change you. It is Dostoevsky's first gift to the world. And like all true gifts, it asks only that you receive it with openness, compassion, and care.

April 8th

My Dearest Barbara Alexievna,

How happy I was last night—so incredibly, so unbelievably happy! It was all because, for once, you decided to grant my request. Around eight o'clock, I woke up from a nap—you know I like to rest for a short while after my work is done. I woke up, lit a candle, prepared my paper to write, and trimmed my pen. Then, for some reason, I happened to glance up—and my heart nearly leapt out of my chest!

You had understood what I wanted, what my heart was longing for. I saw that you had tied up a corner of the curtain on your window, just as I suggested. It felt like your dear face was there at the window, peeking out from the shadows of your room and thinking of me. How I wished I could see your sweet face more clearly! There was a time when it was so easy for us to see each other, wasn't there? But alas, my dearest, age is not always kind.

This morning, my eyes are red and watery from working late last night. Tears stream so much that I feel ashamed to let anyone see me. Yet even without a clear view, I could imagine your bright, kind smile, my angel. The thought filled my heart with the same joy I felt when I first kissed you, my little Barbara. Do you remember that moment? It felt as though, last night, you were playfully wagging your finger at me. Was that the case? You must write and tell me in your next letter.

What do you think of the curtain idea, Barbara? Isn't it wonderful? Whether I'm working, going to bed, or waking up, it lets me know that you're thinking of me and remembering me—that you're well and happy. When you lower the curtain, it means it's time for me to go to bed. And when you raise it, it's like you're saying, "Good morning!" asking how I've slept and telling me, "I'm feeling well, thank God!"

You see, my love, how simple the idea is? And think of how much writing it will save us! It's clever, isn't it? And I came up with it myself! Aren't I clever, Barbara Alexievna?

Let me tell you something else, my dearest. Last night, I slept better and more soundly than I ever thought possible, especially since I've just moved into a new place—a change that usually makes it hard to rest. This morning, I woke up early, feeling joyful and full of love. Everything seemed so fresh and beautiful. When I opened my window, the sun was shining, birds were singing, and the air was filled with the scents of spring. It felt like the whole world was coming back to life.

Everything seemed to match my mood, and I had a strong feeling that today would be a good day. Yet, as I thought of these things, my mind kept returning to you. I wondered why we humans, who endure so much sorrow, cannot be like the birds of the sky, who know no such suffering. My thoughts were full of such comparisons, fanciful though they may seem.

There's a little book I own that says similar things in many different ways. It explains how spring can fill us with pleasant, playful, and tender thoughts. It makes the world look brighter. From that book, I copied a passage for you. The author expresses a longing I feel myself when he writes:

"Why am I not a bird, free to seek my quest?"

He writes many other beautiful things as well—God bless him!

Tell me, my love, where did you go for your walk this morning? Before I left for the office, I saw you leaving your room, walking through the courtyard, looking as fresh as spring itself. It filled me with such joy to see you!

Ah, little Barbara, you mustn't give in to sadness. Tears won't help, nor will sorrow. I know this all too well from my own experience. Take care of yourself and rest until you feel stronger.

And how is our dear Thedora? What a kind heart she has! You wrote that she's now living with you and that you're pleased with her work. True, you mentioned that she grumbles at times, but don't let that bother you. God bless her—she's a good soul!

As for my new home, what a place it is, Barbara Alexievna! It's nothing like the quiet apartment I used to have, where you could hear a fly buzzing. Here, it's noisy, with constant shouting and clattering. Imagine a long, dark corridor lined with doors. Each room is rented out to different tenants—sometimes one, sometimes two or three. It's like a little Noah's Ark.

Most of the lodgers are respectable and well-read. There's a government clerk who knows Homer and can discuss any author you mention. There are also two officers who are always playing cards, a midshipman, and an English tutor.

But I'll tell you more about them in my next letter. For now, let me describe my little space. I live in a small room connected to the kitchen. It's cozy, with just enough room for my bed, a table, a chest of drawers, and two chairs. I even have a window!

Don't misunderstand why I chose this room, my dearest. It's not because I've given up on better things. I simply wanted a comfortable place where I could save a little money. And since your window is directly across from mine, I can see you passing by, which makes this little space feel like paradise.

Goodbye for now, my angel. I've written so much that I should have left for the office long ago. I send you two small pots of geraniums as a gift. Let me know if you'd like some mignonette as well.

Yours always,

Makar Dievushkin

April 8th

My Dearest Makar Alexievitch,

I must scold you. Truly, my kind Makar Alexievitch, I cannot keep accepting your gifts, knowing what they must cost you. I know how much you've sacrificed and how many comforts you've gone without to send them to me. How many times have I told you that I need nothing—absolutely nothing—and that I'll never be able to repay all the kindness you've shown me?

Why, for example, did you send me geraniums? A little sprig of balsam would have been plenty, but geraniums! The moment I casually mention something—like geraniums—you go out and buy it for me! How much must those flowers have cost? Yet they are so beautiful with their bright, fiery petals. Where did you even find such lovely plants? I've placed them in the most prominent spot on my windowsill. I even rearranged my other flowers, putting them on a bench on the floor, to make space.

Unfortunately, Thedora, who is always busy sweeping and tidying, is not entirely pleased with the arrangement. Still, they look wonderful. But why did you also send bonbons? Reading your letter, I could tell there's something on your mind. You wrote so much about paradise, spring, sweet smells, and birdsong that it felt like I was reading poetry! Your letter was so beautiful, Makar Alexievitch, it only lacked verses to be complete.

Your tender feelings, your bright, dreamy thoughts—I could feel them in every word. And about the curtain? I never thought of it! When I moved the flower pots, the curtain looped itself up on its own. That's all there is to it!

Ah, Makar Alexievitch, you say nothing about what you've spent on me. You try to hide it, pretending that the cost is nothing. But I know you deny yourself so much for my sake. Why did you take that tiny, uncomfortable room? It must be noisy and crowded, and you love peace and solitude. Someone like you deserves better. From what Thedora has told me, your situation used to be much better than it is now.

Why should I believe that you've always lived in loneliness, want, and sadness, without a kind word or the comfort of a friend? My heart aches for you, dear friend! Please take care of yourself and your health. You mentioned that your eyes are too weak for writing by candlelight in the office. Why push yourself like that? Surely your superiors already know how dedicated you are.

And please, stop spending so much on me. I know how much you care for me, but I also know you're not rich.

This morning, I woke up feeling cheerful. Thedora was already hard at work, and I felt ready to get moving myself. I went out to buy some silk, then returned home to focus on my sewing. All morning I felt lighthearted. But now, my thoughts have darkened again. My heart feels heavy, and sadness has crept back in.

What will become of me? What is my future? Not knowing what lies ahead weighs so heavily on me. Looking back at the past is no better—it's filled with pain and memories that break my heart. I feel I could cry for a century over the cruelty of those who have ruined my life.

But dusk is falling, and I must return to my work. There's so much more I'd like to write, but I'm running out of time. Writing to you is never a burden; it's always a joy. But why don't you come visit me? You live so close, and surely you can spare some time. Please come, Makar Alexievitch.

I saw Theresa earlier. She looked so unwell that I felt sorry for her and gave her twenty kopecks. Now I'm so tired I can barely keep my eyes open. Write to me soon and tell me everything—how you're living, who your neighbors are, and what they're like. I want to know all about it!

Tonight, I've looped the curtain up on purpose. And please, go to bed early. Last night, I saw your light burning until nearly midnight.

Goodbye for now. I feel so sad and weary. How hard it is to live through days like this. Once more, goodbye.

Your friend,

Barbara Dobroselova

April 8th

My Dearest Barbara Alexievna,

What a day this has been for me! Surely, you're teasing an old man. Still, it's my own fault. I should have known better than to cling to romantic ideas at my age. Naturally, I've been misunderstood. But what a strange creature man can be! He talks about doing things, yet often does nothing and ends up looking foolish. May the Lord keep us from such folly!

I'm not angry, my dear, just upset with myself for writing to you in such flowery, silly words. This morning, I went to the office with a spring in my step because my heart was filled with thoughts of you. It felt like a holiday in my soul. Everything seemed so cheerful at first, but as I settled into my work, I found myself gazing at the same dull objects I see every day—those same old inkstains, tables, and chairs. Why had they seemed different this morning? Why had I been so swept up in my mood?

It must have been because a certain someone brought light into my life, turning my grey skies blue. It's strange how sometimes, even in the most ordinary places, our imagination can trick us into sensing something sweet and beautiful. But as I walked home this evening, my mood changed. My feet felt heavy, my head ached, and a cold wind ran down my back. Foolishly, I had worn only a thin coat because the morning seemed so lovely.

Please don't misunderstand me, dear Barbara. My feelings toward you are not what you think. They are entirely paternal. I see myself as a relative bound to watch over and protect you in your lonely situation. This I say honestly and sincerely, as any family member might. After all, I am a distant relative—if only a small one, as the saying goes. But

I am still your nearest kin and protector now, especially since those who should have cared for you gave you nothing but betrayal and hurt.

As for poetry, I've always thought it's foolish for a man of my years to dabble in verses. Even schoolboys should be scolded for wasting their time on such things.

Why do you ask about my comfort? I've never been one to demand much. Truly, I'm as comfortable now as I've ever been. I have food, warm clothes, and small pleasures to enjoy. My father wasn't a gentleman either, and his family lived even more simply than I do now. Still, I must admit that I miss my old room. It felt cozier somehow, even though my current one has its own advantages.

That old room was where I spent so many quiet years with my kind landlady, who is no longer with us. She was a good woman, always busy making patchwork quilts, and never overcharged for rent. I can't help but think of her granddaughter, Masha, who was just a little girl back then. She must be thirteen now. How that mischievous child used to make us laugh!

Evenings were so peaceful. We'd gather around the big table for tea, then work quietly while the landlady told stories to keep Masha entertained. What stories they were—better suited for adults than children, yet so captivating! Sometimes I'd forget my work entirely just listening to them.

Now, those memories feel so far away. The candle's flickering light, the sound of snow swirling outside—it all seems like a dream. How happy we were in those days, living together like a small family.

But here I am rambling again. Perhaps you find this uninteresting, and I admit it's not easy to dwell on such thoughts. Darkness is falling, Theresa is busy with her tasks, and my head aches. Even my thoughts seem to hurt. Today, my heart feels heavy, Barbara.

You ask why I don't visit you in person. My dear, what would people say? If I were to cross the courtyard to see you, people would start gossiping, twisting things into something they're not. It's better this way. I'll see you tomorrow at Vespers. That will be better for both of us.

Don't be upset with me for this letter. I know it's disorganized and rambling. I'm an old man, dear Barbara, and not very educated. I didn't learn much in my youth, and now things don't stick in my mind the way they should. Writing clearly is hard for me, and when I try, it often turns into nonsense.

I saw you at your window today, pulling down the curtain. Goodbye, my dear Barbara. May God keep you safe. Goodbye, my sweet Barbara Alexievna.

Your sincere friend,

Makar Dievushkin

P.S. Don't think I'd ever write to you in a mocking tone. I'm too old for such foolishness, and people would laugh at me if I did. Remember our saying: "He who digs a pit for someone else often falls into it himself."

April 9th

My Dearest Makar Alexievitch,

Aren't you, my dear friend and protector, just a little ashamed to feel so discouraged and gloomy? And surely you are not upset with me? Oh, how thoughtless my words must have seemed, though I never meant for you to take them as a joke at your expense. Please believe me, I would never mock your age or your character. My carelessness is the only thing to blame—along with how weary I feel with life itself.

What such weariness can lead to! To be honest, I thought you were teasing me in your letter. That made my heart heavy, thinking you might truly be displeased with me. My kind friend and helper, you would be wrong to ever think, even for a moment, that I lack gratitude or care for you. My heart understands and deeply values everything you have done for me—protecting me from my enemies, from hatred, and from cruelty. I will never stop praying for you, Makar Alexievitch. If my prayers ever reach Heaven, I know good fortune will surely come your way!

Today I'm not feeling well. One moment I'm shivering, the next I feel flushed and warm. Thedora is very worried about me.

Don't hesitate to come and see me, Makar Alexievitch. Why should it matter what others think? You and I understand each other, and no one else has any say in our lives.

Goodbye for now, Makar Alexievitch. I've said all I had to say, and I feel too unwell to write more. Once again, please don't be upset with me. Know that I will always respect and care for you.

Your humble and devoted servant,

Barbara Dobroselova

April 12th

Dearest Mistress Barbara Alexievna,

Please, my dear, tell me what is wrong. Every one of your letters worries me deeply. In each reply, I beg you to take better care of yourself, to dress warmly, avoid bad weather, and be cautious in everything you do. Yet you don't listen! Oh, my sweet angel, you are as delicate as a blade of grass, bending at the slightest breeze. You must take care of yourself, my dearest. You have to be careful, or you will bring sadness and despair to those who care about you.

You said you wanted to know about my daily life and surroundings, so let me explain everything to you as clearly as I can. When you first enter this house, you come into a plain, bare hallway, which leads to a narrow staircase. The reception room is bright, clean, and lined with polished wood and metal, but the scullery is filthy, greasy, and smells terrible. The stairs are covered in rags, and the walls are so sticky that your hand gets stuck if you touch them. On every landing, there's a clutter of boxes, chairs, and broken furniture. The windows have broken panes, and tubs full of dirty water, trash, eggshells, and fish bladders stand everywhere. The smell is awful.

I've told you about the layout of the rooms before. They're arranged conveniently enough, but each has its own peculiar smell—a kind of thick, sweet odor that takes some getting used to. At first, it's unpleasant, but after a while, you stop noticing it. However, birds cannot survive here. One naval officer has already lost five canaries. The air just doesn't suit them.

Every morning, the house comes alive with noise as people wake up and get ready for work. Tea is served first, but since the landlady owns only a few tea-urns, everyone has to wait their turn. If you're late, your teapot will be emptied and put away—just as mine was the first day.

I've met most of the people living here. The naval officer was the first to visit me. He told me all about his family and promised to help me if I needed anything. He even invited me for tea. When I went to his room, everyone there was busy playing cards. They tried to get me to join in, but I refused, which made the atmosphere awkward. I stayed quiet while they played all night, and when I left, my eyes ached from the dust and smoke in the room. I won't be going back. Everyone here seems obsessed with gambling.

The landlady is not a pleasant woman. You've seen her before— thin and pale, like a plucked chicken. She and her servant, Phaldoni, handle everything in the house. Phaldoni is rude and quarrels constantly with Theresa, another tenant. Their fights nearly turn into physical brawls. Life here is far from peaceful.

One family stands out, though. They live quietly in a corner room and hardly make a sound. The father, Gorshkov, used to be a government clerk but lost his position years ago. His coat is worse than mine, and he looks so frail that it hurts to see him. His wife and children are no better off. I once heard quiet sobbing from their room. It broke my heart.

Goodbye, my dear Barbara. I've tried to describe everything as best I could. You've been on my mind all day, and my heart longs for you. I know you need a warm cloak, just as I feel the bitter St. Petersburg winds cutting through my thin coat. Forgive me if my writing rambles. I've never had much of an education, but I hope my words bring you a little cheer.

Your faithful and devoted friend,

Makar Dievushkin

April 25th

My Dearest Makar Alexievitch,

Today I ran into my cousin Sasha. Seeing how her life has fallen apart was a terrible shock. I've also heard through others that she has been asking about me and trying to follow me around, pretending she wants to forgive me, forget the past, and rebuild our relationship. Among other things, she told me that you are not truly a relative of mine, that she is my closest family, and that you have no right to involve yourself in our family matters. She said it's wrong and shameful for me to live off your earnings and kindness.

She even claimed I've forgotten all she did for me—that she saved both me and my mother from starvation, fed us, and gave us shelter. She went on to say we caused her great financial loss over two and a half years and that, most importantly, she forgave the debt we owed her. Not even my late mother was spared from her accusations. If only my poor mother could see from her grave how I'm being treated! But God knows the truth.

Anna also said it's entirely my fault that my situation worsened after she supposedly helped me. She insists she's not to blame for what happened and that I'm the only one responsible for failing to protect my own honor. Great God! Who, then, is at fault? According to Anna, Mr. Bwikov was right to refuse to marry me, claiming that—Oh, why should I repeat such cruel lies? It's too painful to even write this. What will happen to me now, I don't know. I tremble, cry, and sob uncontrollably. It's taken me two hours just to finish this letter.

One would think Anna might at least admit her share of responsibility for what happened in the past. But look at what she says instead! It's unbearable.

22

Please, for the love of God, don't worry too much about me, my friend, my only supporter. Thedora tends to exaggerate everything. I'm not seriously ill; I've just caught a slight cold. I got it last night while walking to Bolkovo to hear Mass for my mother. Oh, my poor mother! If only you could rise from your grave and see what's being done to your daughter!

B.D.

May 20th

My Dearest Little Barbara,

I'm sending you some grapes—they're supposed to be very good for someone recovering from illness, and doctors often recommend them for reducing fever. You also mentioned recently that you'd like some roses, so I'm sending you a small bouquet. Are you managing to eat anything, my love? That's the most important thing for you to focus on right now. Let's thank God that the worst is behind us and that things are looking better. Yes, let's be grateful for that!

As for books, I haven't been able to find any except one that people say is written beautifully and highly praised. I've borrowed it to read myself—would you like me to send it to you as well? Though, honestly, I feel a little unsure about what kind of books you'd enjoy. Based on what I know about you, maybe you'd like poetry—something emotional and romantic? If so, I could send you some of my own poems. I've already started copying out part of the manuscript.

Everything is going well for me, so please don't worry about me, my dearest. What Thedora told you was nothing but nonsense. Please tell her from me that she's spreading falsehoods. No, I haven't sold a new uniform, as she claimed. Why would I, when I still have forty roubles left from my salary? So, don't be anxious about me, my darling. Thedora just likes to stir up trouble—she's a vindictive woman, that's all. Better days are coming, I promise. But for now, your only concern should be getting better, my angel. Please recover, for my sake, so you don't cause this old man grief.

And who told you that I'm looking thin? More lies—nothing but lies! In fact, I'm as healthy as ever, and I've even gained so much weight that I'm almost embarrassed about it. I wish you were as healthy as I am!

Goodbye for now, my little angel. I kiss each of your delicate fingers and remain always your devoted friend,

Makar Dievushkin.

P.S.—What is this you've written to me, my dear? Why do you put me on such a pedestal? And how could I visit you so often, as you suggest? How, I ask you? Perhaps I could come under the cover of darkness, but the season doesn't offer much night at all. Besides, I don't even know how I managed to do everything I did during your illness and delirium—I was by your side constantly. Later, I had to stop visiting entirely because people started noticing and asking questions. Even now, a little scandal has arisen. I trust Theresa completely—she isn't someone who talks too much—but imagine the gossip when everything comes out in the open! What will people think and say then?

Still, don't let this trouble you, my love. Focus on getting better, and when you've recovered, we'll find a way to meet outside.

June 1st

My Dearest Makar Alexievitch,

I am so eager to do something that will make you happy, to repay you for all the care and effort you have shown me—for your love and devotion. That is why I decided to spend some time digging through my things to find the manuscript I'm sending you now. I started writing it during a happier time in my life and have worked on it now and then since then. You've asked me so many times about my past—about my mother, about Pokrovski, about my time with Anna Thedorovna, and about the hardships I've faced recently. You've often said you wanted to read this account of my life, so I hope it brings you joy.

Yet, I feel a sadness when I read it now. I feel as though I've aged so much since I finished those final lines. Oh, Makar Alexievitch, I am so tired. This insomnia torments me! Recovery can be such a struggle.

Until I was fourteen, when my father passed away, my childhood was the happiest time of my life. It all began far from here in the Tula province, where my father worked as a steward on the vast estate of Prince P——. We lived in a quiet little village owned by the prince, and our life was simple and peaceful, but full of happiness. I was a carefree child who spent my days running around the fields, woods, and garden. No one paid much attention to me—my father was busy with work, and my mother was always managing the household. No one even bothered to give me lessons, which I didn't mind one bit.

At dawn, I would head out to the pond or the woods or the fields. I loved feeling the sun on me, running wherever I pleased, getting my hands scratched by branches, and tearing my clothes. I would get scolded for it later, but I didn't care.

If I could have stayed in that village forever, I would have been happy all my life. But fate had other plans. We left my childhood home before I had even grown up. I was just twelve years old when we moved to St. Petersburg.

The memories of our departure still hurt me. I remember the sad goodbyes, the tearful farewells, and how I clung to my father, begging him to let us stay just a little longer. He told me to stop, while my mother, crying as well, explained that business required us to leave. Old Prince P—— had passed away, and his heirs dismissed my father from his position. With a small amount of money invested in St. Petersburg, my father decided he needed to be in the city to manage his affairs. My mother was the one who explained all this to me.

We moved to St. Petersburg and stayed there until my father's death. It was so hard for me to adjust to our new life. We arrived in the autumn, a time when the countryside is bright and crisp, with the harvest safely stored, and flocks of birds flying overhead. In the country, it's a joyful time. But in St. Petersburg, all we found was rain, cold winds, dull gray skies, and crowds of unfriendly, sullen people.

Still, we settled in. I remember how noisy and chaotic it was as we tried to set up our new home. After that, my father was rarely home, and my mother was always busy. I felt forgotten.

The first morning after we arrived, I woke up feeling so sad. I looked out of the window and saw only a bleak wall across from us. The street below was dirty, with hardly any people walking by, and those who did were huddled against the cold.

Then came days filled with gloom and sadness. In St. Petersburg, we had almost no relatives or friends. Even my father and Anna Thedorovna had fallen out over money he owed her. The only visitors we had were business callers, who usually came to argue, complain, and cause a fuss. Their visits left my father angry and silent. He would pace the room with a frown, not speaking to anyone. My mother didn't dare approach him, and I would sit quietly in a corner, reading and trying not to draw attention to myself.

Three months after we arrived in St. Petersburg, I was sent to a boarding school. It was a strange and unpleasant place, filled with unfamiliar people. The teachers were harsh, constantly yelling, and the other girls made fun of me. I felt awkward and out of place. The strict rules, the shared meals, and the endless oversight from teachers were overwhelming. I couldn't sleep at night and often cried through the cold, lonely hours. In the evenings, we had to study or memorize lessons, and I would sit there, hunched over a book, too scared to move. My thoughts constantly wandered back to home—my father, my mother, my old nurse, and the stories she used to tell me.

I missed everything about our little home. Memories of the smallest things brought me comfort. I would imagine sitting in our warm, cozy parlor, drinking tea with my parents. In my mind, I would hug my mother so tightly, as though I could make up for all the time away. These thoughts always brought tears to my eyes, and I would struggle to focus on my lessons. No matter how much I studied, I couldn't remember the material by morning. The teachers scolded me, and I was punished with kneeling and given only one meal a day. My classmates teased and mocked me, pinched me on the way to meals, and made false complaints about me to the headmistress.

But how I looked forward to Saturday evenings! That was when my old nurse would come to take me home. I would greet her with such joy, and as we walked home, I would chatter away about everything that had happened during the week. Once I got home, I would throw my arms around my parents, as though we hadn't seen each other in years. Those evenings were filled with laughter, stories, and pure happiness.

My father and I often had serious talks about school, my teachers, and my struggles with French grammar, but overall, we were a happy family. I could see how hard my father worked to support me and how much he sacrificed for my education. This made me try even harder with my lessons, though it didn't always help. Over time, my father grew more irritable and withdrawn. His debts piled up, and his business troubles worsened. My mother, already frail, became quieter and thinner. She developed a painful cough and rarely spoke, fearing to upset my father further.

When I came home from school, I often found the house heavy with sadness. My mother's silent tears, my father's angry words, and the constant arguments made it hard to feel any joy. My father seemed to blame me for everything—for not learning French well enough, for the headmistress's supposed incompetence, even for the money spent on my schooling. The smallest disagreements would escalate into full-blown arguments, often about things I didn't even understand.

Despite all this, I knew my father loved us. His frustrations came from his inability to express that love and to cope with his own troubles. Yet it broke my heart to see how my mother suffered. Her cheeks grew hollow, her eyes sunken, and her face flushed with sickness. It hurt even more to know that I was often the center of the conflict.

My father's worries consumed him, and he neglected his health. One day, he caught a chill, and after a brief illness, he passed away suddenly. The shock was overwhelming. My mother was so stricken with grief that I feared she might lose her mind. As soon as he died, creditors appeared out of nowhere, demanding payment. We lost everything we owned, including the small house my father had bought shortly after we arrived in St. Petersburg. I don't even know how the debts were settled, but we were left with nothing—no home, no money, nothing to live on. My mother was gravely ill, and I was only fourteen.

It was then that Anna Thedorovna came to see us. She introduced herself as a lady of property and a relative—though my mother clarified that the connection was distant. During my father's life, Anna had shown no interest in us, but now she arrived in tears, promising to help. She expressed regret for the past and blamed my father for living beyond his means. She asked for forgiveness and spoke of reconciling with us. My mother, though hesitant, agreed.

Anna even took my mother to church to have a Mass said for my father, calling him the "dear departed." After this display of sorrow, she invited us to visit her home, and though my mother hesitated, she eventually accepted. We had no other choice.

I will never forget the day we moved to Vassilievski Island. It was a crisp, clear autumn morning, but the chill in the air matched the sadness in my heart. My mother cried the whole way, and I felt as though my heart would break under the weight of sorrow. Everything felt so uncertain, so frightening, so unbearably sad.

At first, living at Anna Thedorovna's house felt strange and unpleasant for both my mother and me. The house, which Anna owned, had five rooms. She shared three of them with my orphaned cousin Sasha, whom she had raised since infancy. My mother and I lived in the fourth room, while the fifth was rented by a poor student named Pokrovski. Although Anna lived more lavishly than one might expect, her income and work were a mystery. She was always busy with something secretive and had a constant stream of visitors, though we had no idea who they were or why they came. Whenever the doorbell rang, my mother would quickly take me back to our room. Anna didn't like this and often accused my mother of being too proud for our circumstances. She would sulk for hours about it.

At the time, I didn't understand these accusations. It wasn't until much later that I realized—or guessed—the real reasons behind my mother eventually saying we couldn't stay there anymore. Anna was not a kind person. Though she was polite to us at first, her true nature became clear as soon as she realized we were completely dependent on her and had no other place to go. In the beginning, she even treated me with exaggerated kindness, but later, I suffered as much as my mother did. Anna constantly reminded us of her so-called generosity, often introducing us to her friends as her poor relatives, whom she had taken in out of Christian charity. During meals, she would watch every bite we took, and if we ate too little, she'd start her lectures again. She'd call us picky, tell us riches don't bring happiness, and suggest we should live on our own if we didn't like it.

Anna never stopped criticizing my late father, blaming him for everything. She said he had tried to act superior and ended up ruining his family, leaving us destitute. She claimed that if she hadn't helped us, we would have ended up homeless. Her words weren't just painful— they were disgusting to hear. My mother often broke down in tears, her health deteriorating rapidly as she grew thinner and weaker.

We had to work constantly, taking in sewing jobs from morning until night. Although we desperately needed the money—for clothes, emergencies, and the hope of someday leaving Anna's house—this arrangement didn't please her. She complained that her house wasn't meant to be a workshop. The endless work and stress took a toll on my mother, whose illness grew worse day by day. I could see clearly how much she was suffering, both physically and emotionally, but there was nothing I could do to help.

Our days passed in monotonous quiet, as if we were living in the countryside. Anna seemed to grow calmer as she realized the full extent of her control over us. We didn't dare to challenge her in any way. Our room was separated from hers by a corridor, and next to us lived Pokrovski, the student who tutored Sasha in French, German, history, and geography—or, as Anna proudly put it, "all the sciences." In exchange for teaching Sasha, he received free room and board. Sasha was a bright but rude and wild thirteen-year-old girl.

At one point, Anna suggested to my mother that I should also take lessons, given that my education had been neglected. My mother eagerly agreed, and I began studying with Sasha under Pokrovski for a year. Pokrovski was a poor young man whose fragile health had prevented him from completing a full university education. We called him "The Student" mostly out of formality. He was quiet and humble, rarely making a sound in his room. His appearance was awkward, and the way he spoke was so peculiar that, at first, I couldn't help but laugh when I saw him. Sasha, on the other hand, loved to play pranks on him, especially during lessons.

Unfortunately, Pokrovski was as temperamental as Sasha. The smallest provocation could send him into a fit of frustration. He would shout at us, complain about our behavior, and sometimes storm out of the room before the lesson was over. After such outbursts, he would retreat to his room and spend days buried in his books. His collection of books was both rare and valuable, and whenever he earned money from tutoring at another place, he would immediately spend it on buying more.

In time, I came to know and like him better, as he was truly a kind and decent person—much better than most of the people we usually encountered. My mother respected him greatly, and after her, he became my closest friend. But at first, I was just a silly, mischievous girl, teaming up with Sasha to play pranks on him. We spent hours trying to irritate and distract him because his frustration made him look so amusing, even though I feel ashamed to admit it now. Once, after we had pushed him to the verge of tears, I overheard him mutter to himself, "What cruel children!" That made me feel deeply guilty. I was overcome with sadness and regret, and I immediately begged him, almost crying, not to take our childish jokes seriously or be angry with us. But he didn't finish the lesson. Instead, he quietly closed his book and left for his room.

That entire day, I was wracked with remorse, unable to stop thinking about how we had made him, poor and already burdened, remember his struggles. That night, I couldn't sleep, overwhelmed by guilt and regret. They say remorse eases the soul, but it didn't feel that way to me. I don't know if my guilt was tied to my pride, but I didn't want him to think of me as just a silly child. After all, I was already fifteen. From that moment on, I became determined to show him I was more mature, to change his opinion of me. Yet, being naturally shy and reserved, I couldn't come up with any clear plan, only vague dreams of proving myself. Still, I stopped participating in Sasha's pranks, and in turn, Pokrovski stopped losing his temper with us so often. But even then, I couldn't shake the feeling that I hadn't done enough to earn his respect.

At this point, I need to tell you about one of the most unusual, interesting, and pitiable people I've ever met. I mention him here because, up until this time, I had barely noticed him. But now, because of my growing interest in Pokrovski, I began to pay attention to everything connected to him.

A strange little old man would sometimes visit our house. He was poorly dressed, awkward, gray-haired, and always seemed to carry an air of shame, as if he were constantly burdened by a guilty conscience. His odd behavior—jerky movements and peculiar expressions—made him seem like he wasn't entirely in his right mind. When he arrived, he would hesitate by the window in the hall, as though unsure if he should enter. If someone passed by—whether it was Sasha, me, or a servant—he would wave and gesture, signaling that he wanted to come in. Only when someone acknowledged him by name or nodded would he enter, rubbing his hands with satisfaction and tiptoeing quietly to Pokrovski's room. This strange old man was none other than Pokrovski's father.

33

Later, I learned his story in more detail. He had once been a low-ranking civil servant without any other means of income. After his first wife, Pokrovski's mother, passed away, he remarried a tradesman's daughter who quickly took control of everything and left the household in shambles. His situation became even worse than before. However, fate had been kinder to the younger Pokrovski. A landowner named Bwikov, who had been acquainted with his father, took him under his wing and sent him to school. Bwikov's interest in Pokrovski also stemmed from his past friendship with the boy's late mother, who had once been a servant under Anna Thedorovna's care before marrying Pokrovski's father. At the wedding, Bwikov had given the couple a dowry of five thousand roubles as a gesture of goodwill, though no one seemed to know what happened to that money.

Pokrovski advanced from school to a gymnasium and eventually to the university, with Bwikov continuing to support him. However, poor health forced him to leave his studies. At that point, Bwikov introduced him to Anna Thedorovna and arranged for him to live at her house, teaching Sasha in exchange for board and lodging.

Meanwhile, Pokrovski's father had descended into despair due to his second wife's harsh treatment. He turned to heavy drinking and spent most of his days in a near-constant state of intoxication. His wife would often beat him or banish him to the kitchen. Over time, he became so used to her abuse and neglect that he stopped complaining. Despite everything, his love for his son remained his only sign of humanity. Pokrovski closely resembled his late mother, which likely fueled his father's deep affection for him, a connection to the loving partner he had lost.

The old man could talk of nothing but his son, whom he visited twice a week without fail. He didn't come more often because the younger Pokrovski didn't welcome these visits. The son's greatest flaw was his lack of respect for his father, though it's fair to say the father wasn't easy to deal with. He was overly curious and often interrupted Pokrovski's work with pointless, rambling questions. Occasionally, he even showed up drunk. Nevertheless, Pokrovski was gradually teaching his father to curb his behavior and regard him as an authority figure, speaking only when given permission.

On the topic of his son, whom he affectionately called Petinka, the poor old man could talk endlessly. Yet, whenever he came to visit, his face always showed a hesitant, worried expression, as if unsure of how he would be received. He would often linger outside the door for a long time, and if I happened to be there, he would spend twenty minutes questioning me about Petinka—asking if he was well, what mood he was in, whether he was busy with important work, or perhaps writing or thinking. Only after I had reassured him enough would he finally make up his mind to enter. Gently, he would open the door, peek his head in, and if his son gave him a nod of approval, he would step inside quietly. He would take off his scarf and hat—an old, battered one full of holes with a crumpled brim—without making a sound. Then, he would carefully sit down on a chair, keeping his eyes fixed on his son, studying his every move to gauge his mood.

If the son seemed upset or in low spirits, the father would notice immediately. He would rise, explain softly that he had "just stopped by for a minute" while out walking, and quietly leave. He would take up his scarf and hat again, open the door without a sound, and leave with a forced smile on his face, trying to hide his disappointment. But when the son received him warmly, the old man's joy was unmistakable. His face would light up, his every gesture would show satisfaction, and he would sit up straighter in his chair. If the son started a conversation, the father would lean forward slightly, answering in a soft, reverent tone while trying to use fancy words—though often his attempts only ended up being awkward or ridiculous.

The poor old man struggled to find the right words, often blushing and fumbling with his hands in embarrassment. After speaking, he would quietly repeat his words to himself, as though trying to justify them. If he managed to say something clever, he would sit back, puff out his chest, and adjust his clothes with an air of pride. Feeling encouraged, he might even get up, casually walk to the bookshelf, and pretend to browse a book as though he were entirely at ease in his son's space. But I remember one time when his son sternly told him not to touch the books. The old man went pale, replaced the book in the wrong position in his nervous hurry, and then awkwardly corrected himself with a forced smile, trying to recover from the rebuke.

Gradually, the younger Pokrovski helped his father change his ways. He promised him small coins as a reward if he came to visit sober three times in a row. Occasionally, he even bought his father small gifts, like shoes, a tie, or a waistcoat. Each time, the old man would beam with pride over his new possession, showing it off like it was the most precious treasure. Sometimes, he would stop by to see Sasha and me, bringing us little treats like gingerbread birds or apples. He always spoke highly of Petinka, calling him a good and brilliant son, and encouraging us to work hard on our lessons. He would wink at us in a playful way, twisting and turning in such an amusing fashion that we couldn't help but laugh. My mother liked him a lot, though he couldn't stand Anna Thedorovna and stayed very subdued in her presence.

Shortly after this, I stopped taking lessons with Pokrovski. He still thought of me as a child, just as immature as Sasha, and this hurt me deeply, especially after all my efforts to redeem myself for past behavior. It felt like my attempts to change had gone unnoticed, and the more I thought about it, the more it upset me. I barely spoke to him outside of lessons because I felt too self-conscious. If I tried to talk to him, I would blush, lose my nerve, and end up running off to cry in frustration. I don't know how long this would have gone on if not for an unusual event that changed things.

One evening, while my mother was visiting Anna Thedorovna, I tiptoed to Pokrovski's room, thinking he wasn't home. Something strange compelled me to go. Although we lived so close, I had never seen his room before, and my heart was pounding so hard it felt like it would burst. When I stepped inside, I looked around with intense curiosity. The room was sparsely furnished and untidy, with books and papers scattered everywhere. As I gazed at the shelves, a thought struck me, and with it came a wave of irritation and sadness. It felt as though my friendship and affection meant nothing to him because he was educated, while I was ignorant and had never read a single book.

I stared at the heavy-laden shelves, filled with grief and frustration. I decided then and there that I would read every single one of those books, no matter how long it took, to make myself worthy of his respect. Without thinking further, I grabbed the first dusty book I could reach and pressed it to my chest, trembling with excitement and fear. My plan was to read it secretly by candlelight while my mother slept.

But when I got back to my room and opened it, I was crushed to find it was an old, worm-eaten book in Latin—a language I didn't understand. Frustrated, I returned to put it back. Just as I was fumbling to slide the book back into place, I heard footsteps approaching in the corridor. In my haste, I accidentally knocked the whole shelf loose. The rusty nail holding it in place broke, and the shelf crashed down, spilling books everywhere. At that moment, the door opened, and Pokrovski walked in.

I must mention that Pokrovski hated having his belongings disturbed, especially his books. Imagine my horror when books of all sizes and shapes tumbled from the shelf, scattering across the table, under the chairs, and all over the room. I wanted to run away, but it was too late. "This is it," I thought. "I've ruined everything! How could I have been so foolish, acting like a silly little child? What an absolute fool I am!"

Pokrovski was furious. "What have you done?" he exclaimed. "Aren't you ashamed of always pulling these stunts? Are you ever going to grow up?" He rushed forward to gather the books, and I bent down to help him.

"You don't need to help," he snapped. "It would have been better if you hadn't come in uninvited."

As I lowered my eyes in shame, his tone softened slightly, and he began to speak like a teacher lecturing a student. "When will you learn to be more sensible and serious? Think about it—you're not a little girl anymore; you're fifteen, practically a young woman."

He glanced at me, probably to confirm his point, but then suddenly turned red, as if embarrassed. I couldn't understand why and just stared at him in confusion. Then he straightened up, hesitated, and awkwardly muttered something that might have been an apology for not noticing sooner that I wasn't a child anymore. At that moment, I realized what had caused his reaction. Overcome with embarrassment, I blushed even more deeply than he did, covered my face with my hands, and fled the room.

I didn't know what to do with myself after that. I was overwhelmed with shame, mostly because I had been caught in his room. For three days, I couldn't bring myself to look him in the eye. Every time I saw him, my face burned with embarrassment, and I felt on the verge of tears. My mind was full of confusing, jumbled thoughts. At one point, I even considered going to him, confessing everything, and explaining that I hadn't acted out of mischief but with honest intentions. I wanted to tell him everything and beg his forgiveness. But I couldn't summon the courage. Even now, the thought of doing so makes me cringe.

A few days later, my mother became gravely ill. For two days, she couldn't leave her bed, and by the third night, she was delirious with fever. I had stayed up the previous night, tending to her every need—bringing her water, giving her medicine at the right times, and keeping watch by her side. By the next night, I was utterly exhausted. Sleep kept pulling at me, and everything around me blurred. My head spun, and I felt like I might faint from sheer fatigue. Yet every time my mother moaned softly, I snapped back to alertness, only to be overcome by drowsiness again moments later. It was unbearable.

I can't remember everything clearly, but at one point, I think I dozed off and had a horrible dream. I woke up in a panic. The room was dimly lit; the candle flickered, casting strange shadows on the walls before plunging the room back into semi-darkness. A heavy sense of fear and unease gripped me. My heart felt weighed down, and I could hardly breathe. Suddenly, I jumped up from my chair and let out a cry—an uncontrollable burst of terror and frustration.

Just then, the door opened, and Pokrovski stepped in. The next thing I knew, I was in his arms. He gently set me down on a bench, gave me a glass of water, and asked me a few questions. I don't remember how I answered him. "You're not well yourself," he said, taking my hand. "You have a fever, and you're exhausting yourself by neglecting your own health. You need to rest. Lie down and sleep, even if only for a little while. Go on, lie down."

Too tired to argue, I stretched out on the bench, intending only to rest for half an hour. But I slept until morning. When I woke, Pokrovski was there to tell me it was time to give my mother her medicine.

The following evening, around eight o'clock, I felt somewhat rested and resolved not to fall asleep again while watching over my mother. Just as I was settling into my chair, Pokrovski knocked on the door.

When I opened it, he explained that he had brought me some books to read, thinking they might help pass the time. I accepted them, though I don't even know what they were or whether I ever opened them. That night, I couldn't sleep. A strange excitement kept me restless. I moved constantly, unable to stay in one spot for long.

It wasn't the books but the thought of Pokrovski's concern for me that filled me with a warm, uplifting feeling. I stayed awake until dawn, my mind racing with thoughts of him. Though I was certain he wouldn't return that night, I couldn't help but imagine what he might do if he came to check on me the next evening.

That evening, after everyone else in the house had gone to bed, Pokrovski opened his door and started a conversation with me from the doorway. Though I can't recall exactly what we talked about, I remember feeling flustered, embarrassed, and annoyed with myself. I had waited all day for this moment, dreaming about it and planning what I would say, but when it finally happened, I just wished it would end quickly. Still, that night marked the beginning of our friendship, and during the nights of my mother's illness, we spent hours talking together. Slowly, I broke through his reserve, though each conversation left me frustrated with myself. Yet, at the same time, I felt proud and excited to see him becoming less absorbed in his books because of me.

Eventually, we joked about the incident with the fallen shelf. The timing was perfect because I was feeling unusually open and honest that night. With my emotions heightened, I confessed everything to him—how I wanted to learn, to understand, to grow, and how I hated being treated like a child. I admitted my feelings for him, my desire to be his friend, and my wish to comfort him and make his life easier. He looked at me with a mix of confusion and surprise but said nothing. His silence hurt me deeply, and I started to think he hadn't understood me or, worse, that he might be mocking me. Overcome with disappointment, I burst into tears, unable to stop myself. He grabbed my hand, kissed it, and held it against his chest, trying to comfort me with kind words. Though I can't remember exactly what he said, his efforts filled me with joy. I laughed and cried all at once, blushing with happiness. Even so, I could sense he still felt uneasy and unsure about my intense emotions and the depth of my affection.

At first, he seemed bewildered by my enthusiasm, but eventually, he accepted my feelings with the same simple honesty I had shown. He responded with warmth and kindness, treating me like a friend or even a sister. My heart overflowed with happiness. I had hidden nothing from him, and with each day, we grew closer.

We talked about everything during those bittersweet but wonderful nights. Sitting by the dim glow of the lamp near my mother's bed, we spoke about whatever came to mind, pouring out our hearts and sharing our thoughts. Those hours were both painful and joyful, a mixture of grief and delight. To this day, those memories are bittersweet. They bring both pain and comfort, like a refreshing drop of dew on a wilting flower after a hot day. They remind me of a time when my heart felt alive despite the sorrow.

As my mother began to recover, our midnight conversations came to an end. We exchanged only a few words now and then—brief and seemingly unimportant—but I treasured each one. I found joy in assigning hidden meanings to his words and cherishing their secret value. My life felt complete, and I was content, quietly happy. Several peaceful weeks passed.

One day, the elder Pokrovski came to visit. He was cheerful and talkative, joking and sharing stories. Finally, he explained the reason for his good mood: in a week, it would be his son's birthday. He announced that he planned to celebrate by wearing a new jacket and shoes his wife would buy him and by visiting his son. The old man's happiness was infectious as he chattered away about anything and everything.

The news of Pokrovski's upcoming birthday filled me with excitement. I decided I wanted to give him a gift to remind him of our friendship. But what could I give him? After much thought, I settled on books, knowing he had long wanted a complete set of Pushkin's works in the latest edition. I had saved thirty roubles from my sewing work, money I had intended to spend on a new dress. Eagerly, I sent our cook, Matrena, to find out the price.

To my dismay, the books and binding would cost at least sixty roubles—far more than I had. I didn't know what to do. I didn't want to ask my mother for help because that would mean everyone in the house would know about my gift. Worse, it would make the present seem like payment for his help with my studies, but I wanted the gift to be personal and heartfelt, given without obligation. I wanted to remain in his debt, offering only my friendship in return. Finally, after much deliberation, I came up with a plan.

I knew that at the Gostiny Dvor marketplace, it was sometimes possible to buy books—some nearly new—for half their usual price, provided one bargained hard enough. So, I decided to go there. As it happened, both Anna Thedorovna and we needed a few things the next day, and since my mother was unwell and Anna unwilling to go, it fell to me to handle the errands. Matrena accompanied me on the trip.

I was lucky to quickly find a handsome set of Pushkin's works. I began negotiating right away. At first, the seller asked for more than a shop would have charged, but after much effort, and a few pretend attempts to walk away, I managed to bring him down to ten silver roubles. I felt so proud of myself for haggling successfully! Poor Matrena couldn't understand my enthusiasm or why I wanted to buy books so badly. But then, disaster struck. As soon as the seller noticed that my money included thirty roubles in paper notes, he refused to honor our deal. He insisted on the original price. After much pleading, he finally reduced it a little, but not enough—I was still two and a half roubles short. I could have cried from frustration. Just then, an unexpected event saved me.

Not far away, I spotted the elder Pokrovski. He was surrounded by four or five booksellers who were overwhelming him with their wares. They shoved all sorts of books at him, but he didn't seem to know what he wanted. The poor man looked completely lost, as though he were being scolded. I walked over to him and asked what he was doing. He brightened immediately, clearly happy to see me.

"I'm buying books, Barbara Alexievna," he explained. "They're for Petinka's birthday. He loves books, so I thought I'd get him some."

Pokrovski always spoke in a roundabout way, and now he was even more flustered than usual. Every book he asked about was priced far beyond what he could afford. He would look longingly at the bigger, more expensive volumes, turning them over in his hands before reluctantly putting them back. "No, no, that's too much," he muttered. "I'll try somewhere else." Then he would pick up smaller items like almanacs or collections of poetry.

"Why are you looking at these?" I asked. "They're not worth buying."

"No, no!" he insisted. "These are fine books! See how nice they are!" But his voice wavered, and I could tell he was on the verge of tears. A single tear had already rolled down his pale cheek and reddened nose. I asked how much money he had, and he hesitated before pulling out a small bundle wrapped in dirty newspaper. Inside were a few silver coins and twenty kopecks in copper.

Without a second thought, I grabbed his money and dragged him to the seller I'd been dealing with. "Look here," I told the man. "These eleven volumes of Pushkin are priced at thirty-two and a half roubles. I have thirty, and he has two and a half. Together, we'll buy them as a shared gift."

The elder Pokrovski was overjoyed. He handed over his money eagerly, and the seller bundled the books together for him. Stuffing them into his pockets and carrying the rest in his arms, Pokrovski shuffled off with his prize, promising to bring the books to me the next day.

The following day, he visited his son as usual, staying with him for about an hour. Then he came to see us, his face full of an almost comical expression of secrecy and pride. Beaming with satisfaction, he announced that he had smuggled the books into our kitchen and hidden them in a corner under Matrena's care. From there, the conversation naturally turned to the upcoming birthday. The old man began to talk excitedly about gifts, but it was clear he was struggling to say something. He grew more restless and hesitant, fidgeting nervously in his chair.

Finally, he couldn't hold back any longer. "Listen, Barbara Alexievna," he said timidly. "I have an idea. When his birthday comes, you take ten of the books and give them to him as your gift. Then I'll take the eleventh book and give it to him myself. That way, we'll both have something to give him."

"Why don't we just give the books together, Zachar Petrovitch?" I asked.

"Oh, well... very well," he stammered. "Only, I thought..."

He trailed off, blushing with embarrassment. For a moment, he sat in silence, staring at the floor. Then he explained, "You see, I act foolish sometimes. At home, it's cold, and there are... other troubles.

44

It all makes me feel low. When that happens, I sometimes drink too much. Petinka doesn't like it. He gets angry and lectures me. I want to show him I'm trying to change. I've been saving for this book for a long time—ever since I decided to buy him a gift. I don't often have money unless he gives me some. When he sees what I've done, he'll know I spent it for him, to show I'm trying to do better."

My heart ached for the old man as he looked at me with such nervous anticipation. Without hesitation, I made up my mind.

"Here's what we'll do," I said. "You'll give him all the books."

"All of them?" he asked, startled. "Every single one?"

"Yes, all of them," I replied.

"As my gift?" he continued, still unsure.

"Yes, as your gift alone," I confirmed.

Despite my clarity, he seemed unsure and repeated, "As my gift alone?"

"Yes," I assured him again, trying to make it as simple as possible.

For a moment, he stood there reflecting. "Well," he said finally, "that would be wonderful—so wonderful. But what about you, Barbara Alexievna?"

"I won't give him anything," I said.

"What?" he cried, clearly distressed. "You're going to give Petinka nothing? Do you really mean that?"

His concern was so genuine that he seemed ready to abandon his own plan if it meant I would also give a gift. His kind heart touched me deeply. I quickly reassured him.

"I'll have a gift for him too," I explained, "but what's important is that your son is happy, and you are happy. That will make me happy

45

too. In my heart, I'll feel as though I had given the gift myself."

Relieved, the old man's spirits lifted. He stayed with us for a couple of hours, unable to sit still for a moment. He jumped up constantly, laughing, cracking jokes with Sasha, sneaking kisses onto my hands, and even making funny faces at Anna Thedorovna. Eventually, she grew irritated and shooed him out, though his joy was infectious and unmatched by anything I had ever seen before.

On the big day, he arrived promptly at eleven o'clock, fresh from Mass. He wore a carefully mended frock coat, a new waistcoat, and shiny new shoes, while carrying the books in his arms like a treasure. We all gathered for coffee in Anna Thedorovna's parlor, since it was Sunday. The old man began the conversation by declaring that Pushkin was a magnificent poet. Then, somewhat awkwardly, he moved on to a moral lecture about living a proper life. He described how poor choices could ruin a person and proudly declared that he had been working to improve himself. As proof, he revealed that he had been saving up for a long time to buy his son these books.

I couldn't help but laugh and cry at the same time. The old man certainly knew how to spin a story when it suited him! The books were then carried to Pokrovski's room and placed on a shelf. Of course, Pokrovski quickly figured out the truth about them. Nevertheless, the day was merry. The old man stayed for dinner, and we spent the afternoon playing cards and other games. Sasha was full of energy, and I matched her enthusiasm. Pokrovski paid me special attention and kept trying to speak to me alone, though I made sure it didn't happen. It was the happiest day I'd had in four years.

But now, as I write this, my thoughts turn to the painful memories that followed. My hand grows heavy, as though my pen resists recounting the darker chapters of my life. Perhaps that is why I have lingered so long on the happier moments of my past, recalling even the

46

smallest details with such care and affection. Sadly, those days of joy were short-lived, replaced by sorrow so profound that only God knows when it will end.

My hardships began with Pokrovski's illness and death. He fell seriously ill two months after the events I've just described. During those two months, he worked tirelessly to find a stable job, as he had no reliable income. Like many who are gravely ill, he clung to the hope of a long life, even as his condition worsened. He briefly took a tutoring position, though he disliked the work, and his poor health made other jobs, like entering civil service, impossible. His character began to change, becoming darker and more pessimistic as his illness took hold.

When autumn arrived, he continued his job search, venturing out daily in just a light jacket. Repeated exposure to the cold rain left him bedridden, and he never recovered. He passed away in late October.

During his illness, I hardly ever left his side. I cared for him through long, sleepless nights, offering whatever comfort I could. At times, he was delirious, speaking incoherently about his work, his books, his father, and even me. In these moments, I learned things about his life that I had never known. In the early days of his sickness, others in the house looked at me with suspicion, and even Anna Thedorovna would give me knowing nods. However, I always met their gazes calmly, and eventually, they stopped interfering. Even my mother ceased to object.

Sometimes, Pokrovski recognized me, but more often, he was unaware of my presence. On his final night, his fever and pain were unbearable, and his incoherent murmurs filled the small, dark room like echoes from a crypt. The sound was haunting. Everyone in the house grew anxious, and even Anna began praying for his suffering to end. When the doctor arrived, he solemnly predicted that Pokrovski would not survive the night.

That night, the elder Pokrovski stayed in the corridor outside his son's room. Though we gave him a mattress to lie on, he spent most of the night running in and out of the room. He was so consumed by grief that he looked like a shadow of himself, as if he had lost all awareness of his surroundings. His head trembled with anguish, and his whole body shook as he murmured to himself, as if debating something only he could understand. I was terrified he might lose his mind completely. Just before dawn, he finally collapsed onto the mattress, exhausted from his torment, and fell asleep like a man who had been beaten down. By eight o'clock, however, his son was near death, and I hurried to wake him.

When the elder Pokrovski entered the room, the dying man was fully conscious and said goodbye to all of us. I couldn't cry, though it felt like my heart was breaking into pieces.

The final moments were unbearable. For a while, Pokrovski had been trying to say something, but his failing voice made his words impossible to understand. My heart ached as I watched him struggle. Then, for nearly an hour, he lay quietly, only glancing at me now and then with a sorrowful look and trying to move his cold hands to make some kind of sign. Finally, in a hoarse, weak voice, he attempted his request again, but the sounds were so faint and broken that I still couldn't make out what he wanted. Desperate to help, I brought each person in the house to his bedside and gave him something to drink, but he only shook his head with a look of sorrow.

At last, I realized what he was asking for—he wanted me to open the curtains and let in the light. He must have wanted to take one last look at the world, the sunlight, and life itself. I drew back the curtains, but the scene outside was as gray and dreary as his fading life. The day was overcast, the sky heavy with clouds that seemed to drape the world in a veil of mourning. A light rain streaked the windows, tracing cold, dirty trails of water down the glass. Only a dim, pale light made its way into the room, mingling with the faint glow of the ikon lamp. Pokrovski looked at me, nodded faintly, and then passed away.

Anna Thedorovna arranged the funeral. She purchased a simple coffin and hired a shabby hearse, securing the costs by claiming the dead man's books and belongings. However, the elder Pokrovski fought her fiercely for the books. In his desperate grief, he stuffed his pockets and even his hat with as many as he could carry. For three days, he refused to let the books out of his sight, even taking them to church. It was as though he had lost all sense of reason. He busied himself around the bier with obsessive care, adjusting the candlestick on his son's chest, snuffing out and relighting candles, as though he couldn't focus on any one thing for long.

Neither my mother, who was ill, nor Anna Thedorovna, who was at odds with the elder Pokrovski, attended the requiem. Only the father and I were there. As the service went on, I was gripped by an overwhelming sense of dread and foreboding. My legs felt weak, and it was all I could do to stay upright. When the coffin was finally closed and carried out, I followed the procession only as far as the end of the street. There, the driver picked up speed, and the old man began to run after the hearse, crying loudly. His sobs broke into uneven gasps as he struggled to keep up, his ragged breath interrupted by the movement of his running.

At one point, he lost his hat, but he didn't stop to retrieve it, even though the rain lashed his bare head, and the wind stung his face with sleet. He ran back and forth alongside the hearse, his old greatcoat flapping like wings. Books stuck out of every pocket, and in his hands, he clutched a large volume tightly against his chest. Passersby crossed themselves as the procession passed, some stopping to stare in amazement at the poor, grieving old man. Occasionally, a book would fall from one of his pockets into the mud, and someone would stop him to point it out. Each time, he would pick it up and resume his desperate chase.

At the corner of the street, a tattered old woman joined him, and together they followed the hearse until it turned the corner and disappeared from view. I turned back, overwhelmed with grief. When I reached home, I threw myself into my mother's arms, clinging to her as though she were the only thing anchoring me to life. I kissed her amid a storm of tears, holding her as if by holding on to her, I could keep death itself at bay. Yet, even then, I knew that death was already looming over her.

June 11th

How grateful I am for our walk to the Islands yesterday, Makar Alexievitch! Everything was so fresh, so full of life, and so beautifully green! I hadn't seen anything like it in such a long time. During my illness, I often thought I would never recover, that I was surely going to die. Imagine how I felt yesterday, being outside again! It's true, though, that I might have seemed a little sad at times, and I hope you're not upset with me for that. Even though I was happy and carefree, there were moments when, for reasons I couldn't explain, a wave of sadness would wash over me. I cried over the smallest things and didn't even know why.

The truth is, I still feel unwell, and it makes me see everything in a darker light. The pale, clear sky, the setting sun, the peaceful stillness of the evening—all these things, instead of comforting me, seemed to weigh on my heart. I felt overwhelmed, like my heart was full and needed to spill over in tears. But why am I writing this to you? It's so hard for me to put into words what I'm feeling, yet I find it even harder to keep it inside. Maybe you'll understand me. Tears and laughter—it's all mixed together in my heart.

How kind you are, Makar Alexievitch! Yesterday, you looked at me as if you could see everything I was feeling, as if my happiness made you happy too. Whether it was a cluster of trees, a path, or a sparkling stretch of water, you would stop and point it out to me, as if you were proudly showing me treasures of your own. It showed me what a good and caring soul you have, and I love you for it.

Today, I'm not feeling well again. Yesterday, I got my feet wet, and now I've caught a bit of a chill. Thedora isn't feeling well either. Both of us are under the weather. Please don't forget about me. Come to see me as often as you can.

Yours always,

Barbara Alexievna.

June 12th.

My dearest Barbara Alexievna,

I thought you might write about our day together in a poem, but instead, I received just one sheet of your lovely writing. Even so, I must say that what you wrote, short as it was, is expressed with such beauty and grace. Your descriptions of nature, your reflections on the countryside, and the way you share your feelings—all of it is wonderful. I wish I could write like you! No matter how much I try or how many pages I fill, my words never come out right. It feels like I might as well not write at all. I've learned this about myself over time.

You say that I'm kind and good, that I would never harm anyone, and that I can appreciate the goodness of God reflected in nature. Maybe that's true, my dear. Perhaps I am just as you describe. But if so, it's only because letters like yours soften my heart and fill me with deeper, more meaningful thoughts. Listen, my dearest; I have something to tell you, something I've never shared before.

Let me start from the beginning, from the time I was seventeen and first joined the civil service. Now, I've been working for nearly thirty years. At first, I was so proud of my uniform. As I got older, I began to understand more about life and the people around me. I tried to live honestly and do the right thing. But, my dear, that only led to me being mistreated. You might find it hard to believe, but it's true—people were cruel to me, even though I've always tried to be kind and peaceful.

At first, it was little things: "This is your fault, Makar Alexievitch." Then it became: "Of course, it's Makar Alexievitch's fault." Eventually, I became the scapegoat for everything. No matter what went wrong, it was always blamed on me. I became a joke in the office. People criticized my clothes, my boots, even my appearance. Nothing about me seemed good enough for them. And yet, I never did anything to harm anyone. I never schemed or tried to advance myself unfairly. My only mistake was asking for a raise a few times, but even then, I asked politely.

Still, my dear, none of that matters as long as you think I'm worthy of respect. Your opinion of me is what I treasure most. You are the kindest and most wonderful person I know, and your words give me strength.

You asked me once what I think is the greatest virtue in life. Some people might say it's the ability to make money. Others might joke that the most important thing is not to become a burden to anyone. But, my dear, I've never been a burden to anyone. I earn my own living, even if it's a modest one. My crust of bread may be small, but it's mine, and I've worked hard for it.

Yes, I know people look down on me because I'm just a copyist, an amanuensis. But what's wrong with that? My handwriting is neat and legible, and my work is good enough for important documents. Even His Excellency is satisfied with it. True, I may lack the style to rise higher in my career, but I've done my best, and I'm proud of the work I've done.

My dearest, I hope you'll answer the questions I send in my letters. It would mean so much to me. I want to help you in any way I can, and I know that you need me just as much as I need you. Even if people think I'm insignificant, I don't care, as long as I can be of use to you.

Forgive me for rambling, my dear. I didn't mean to go on like this, but it feels good to speak the truth sometimes. Goodbye for now, my sweet little comforter. I'll come to see you soon, and I'll bring a book with me. Until then, take care of yourself.

Yours always,

Makar Dievushkin

June 20th.

My dearest Makar Alexievitch,

I'm writing to you as quickly as I can because I have something urgent to tell you. There's an opportunity for you to make a great purchase. Thedora says that a retired civil servant she knows is selling a uniform. It's in good condition, follows the official regulations, and is being offered for a very low price. Now, don't tell me you don't have the money, because I know you do. You've said so yourself! Please, use that money and don't save it away. Just look at what you're wearing—those clothes are disgraceful, patched everywhere! You don't have anything decent or new. I know this for a fact, no matter what you might say. So, for once, listen to me and buy this uniform. Do it for me. Show me that you truly care about me.

You've sent me some linen as a gift, but listen, Makar Alexievitch—you're ruining yourself. Why are you spending so much money on me? It's ridiculous how much you're spending. You're being wasteful! I don't need these things. It's unnecessary for you to spend this way. I already know you love me, so there's no need to remind me with gifts. Honestly, I don't like receiving them because I know how much they must have cost you. Please, use your money more wisely. I'm begging you to do so.

You've also asked me to continue writing my memoirs and finish them, but I don't know how I managed to write as much as I did before. I don't have the strength to write more about my past, and I don't want to think about it. Those memories are too painful for me. The hardest part is remembering my poor mother, who left me, her helpless daughter, to be taken advantage of by cruel people. My heart feels like it's bleeding whenever I think about it. The memories are so vivid that

56

I can't push them away, even though a whole year has passed since it all happened. But you already know all this.

I've also told you about what Anna Thedorovna is planning now. She accuses me of being ungrateful and denies the things that have been said about her and Monsieur Bwikov. She keeps sending for me, telling me I've gone astray, but promises that if I return to her, she'll sort everything out with Bwikov and force him to admit his wrongdoing. She even claims he wants to give me a dowry. I want nothing to do with any of them! I'm happy here with you and kind Thedora, who cares for me like my old nurse did—may she rest in peace.

You may only be a distant relative, but I ask you to always defend my honor. As for the others, I don't want to see them or think about them ever again. If only I could forget them completely. What do they want from me now? Thedora thinks it's all just a trick and believes they'll leave me alone eventually. I pray to God that she's right.

B.D.

57

June 21st.

My dearest, my darling,

I want to write to you, but I don't know where to start. Everything feels so strange, almost as if we were living together. I must tell you, I have never had days as happy as the ones I'm experiencing now. It's like God has blessed me with a home and a family of my own! Yes, you are my precious little daughter, my beloved.

But why do you bring up the four measly roubles I sent you? You needed them—I know this from Thedora herself—and it brings me so much joy to be able to help you. Making you happy will always be my greatest pleasure in life. Please, let me have that happiness, and don't try to deny it to me. Things aren't as bad as you think. I feel like I've stepped into the sunshine. First, because I'm living so close to you that it feels like I'm almost with you, which brings great comfort to me. And second, because my neighbor, Rataziaev—the retired official who hosts those literary gatherings—has invited me to tea today. This evening, I'll be attending a gathering to discuss literature! Imagine that, my darling!

Well, goodbye for now. I'm writing this without much purpose, other than to let you know how I'm doing. I got your message through Theresa about needing an embroidered cloak to wear, so I'll go out and buy one for you. Yes, tomorrow I'll purchase that embroidered cloak, and it will make me so happy to fulfill one of your wishes. I already know where to find such a garment.

For now, I remain your sincere friend,

Makar Dievushkin.

June 22nd.

My dearest Barbara Alexievna,

I must tell you about a very sad event that happened in this house today—something that would move anyone to pity. Early this morning, around five o'clock, one of Gorshkov's children passed away from scarlet fever or something similar. I went to visit the family to offer my condolences and found them in terrible poverty and disarray. It's no wonder, considering they live in just one small room, with only a screen for privacy.

The coffin was already there in the room—a plain but decent one, which they had bought ready-made. They told me the child was a boy of nine, a bright and promising little one. What a heartbreaking sight it was! The mother wasn't crying, but she looked utterly broken by grief. Perhaps, in a way, having one less mouth to feed will ease their burden, though they still have two children left—a baby who is still nursing and a little girl about six years old.

It was painful to see the children suffering, knowing there's no way to help them. The father sat on an old, broken chair, wearing a dirty and tattered frock coat. Tears were streaming down his face—not only from sorrow but also because of an eye condition he has suffered from for a long time. He looked so thin and frail. Whenever someone speaks to him, his face turns red, and he becomes too embarrassed and confused to respond.

The little girl, their daughter, was standing beside the coffin. Her face was so serious and thoughtful—too serious for a child so young. It breaks my heart to see a child look so burdened. On the floor lay a rag doll, but she wasn't playing with it. She just stood there silently, with her finger pressed to her lips, not even touching the bonbon the

59

landlady had given her.

Isn't it all just so sad, Barbara?

Makar Dievushkin

June 25th.

My dearest Makar Alexievitch,

I am returning your book. In my opinion, it's not a good one, and I'd rather not keep it. Why do you save your money to buy such useless things? Do books like this honestly interest you, or are you just joking? Anyway, you've now promised to send me something else to read, and I'm willing to share the cost of it.

Goodbye for now, until we see each other again. I have nothing more to add.

B.D.

June 26th.

My dearest Barbara,

"What is this, my dear?" he said. "Surely you've prepared the samovar for some special guest?" Then he gave her a playful tap on the cheek.

What do you think of that, Barbara? Yes, it's a bit bold, but isn't it powerful and moving? Let me share something else with you from Rataziaev's story, Ermak and Zuleika:

"'Do you love me, Zuleika? Tell me again—do you love me?'

"'I do love you, Ermak,' Zuleika whispered.

"'Then thank heaven and earth!' Ermak exclaimed. 'You've made me so happy! You've given me everything my tortured soul has been searching for all these years. You brought me here, my guiding star, to the Girdle of Stone for this moment! I'll show you to the whole world, Zuleika, and no man, demon, or monster will stop me! If only people understood the depths of your tender heart and saw the poetry in each tear you shed. Let me kiss away those tears! Let me cherish those heavenly drops, my love, who isn't even of this earth!'

"'Ermak,' Zuleika said, 'the world is cruel, and people are unfair. But let them drive us away, let them judge us! What does their cold, judgmental world mean to a poor girl like me, raised in the icy wilds of Siberia? They'll never understand me, my darling, my love.'

"'They don't understand?' Ermak cried, his eyes blazing with fury. 'Then the swords of the Cossacks will sing over their heads!'"

Can you imagine how Ermak felt when he found out Zuleika had been killed? While he was away, her blind father, Kouchoum, snuck into Ermak's tent at night to kill the man who had taken his power but accidentally killed his own daughter instead.

"'Oh, if I had a stone to sharpen my blade!' Ermak cried in his rage, trying to hone his sword on an enchanted rock. 'I will have his blood! I'll tear him apart for this!'"

Unable to bear the loss of Zuleika, Ermak threw himself into the Irtisch River, and that was the end of the story.

Here's another little piece—this one's meant to be funny:

"Do you know Ivan Prokofievitch Zheltopuzh? He's the man who bit a chunk out of Prokofi Ivanovitch's leg. Ivan is a rough character, not particularly virtuous, but he has a great love for radishes and honey. He once had a friend named Pelagea Antonovna. Do you know her? She's the woman who always wears her petticoat inside out."

Isn't that hilarious, Barbara? We couldn't stop laughing when Rataziaev read it aloud. That's the kind of writer he is. Sure, it's a bit silly, but it's harmless fun, without any controversial ideas.

Sometimes, I wonder—what if I wrote something myself? What if a book appeared with the title The Poetical Works of Makar Dievushkin? What would you think of that, my angel? I'd be too embarrassed to go out in public. Imagine people saying, "Look, there's the writer Dievushkin!" How could I handle that? Especially with my patched shoes! What if a duchess or a countess noticed me? Though, maybe they wouldn't even care.

But enough of my rambling. I just wanted to amuse you and lift your spirits. Goodbye for now, my angel. I'm sending you a long letter because I'm in good spirits after dining with Rataziaev. I'll bring you a new book soon—but not the one I just read. It was by Paul de Kock, and it's not something you should read. Instead, I'm sending you some sweets. Whenever you eat one, think of me. Be careful with the iced ones—suck them slowly so they don't hurt your teeth. Let me know if you like them, and I'll send more.

Goodbye, my dear. May Christ watch over you always!

Your faithful friend,

Makar Dievushkin

June 27th.

My dearest Makar Alexievitch,

Thedora has told me that some people she knows can help me get a good job as a governess in a certain household. What do you think about that, my friend? Should I go? If I accept, I wouldn't have to depend on you anymore, and the position seems like it could be comfortable. But at the same time, the idea of moving into a strange house frightens me. The family are landowners, and they would surely ask me all kinds of questions and try to get involved in my life. What would I even say to them? You see, I've grown so unused to being around people—I'm so shy now. I prefer staying in the familiar little corner I've become used to. A place you know, even if it's filled with sadness, is still the best place.

I have no idea what this job might require. Perhaps they'd expect me to act as more of a nursemaid than a governess. And besides, I've heard that in the past two years, three governesses have come and gone from that house. Please, Makar Alexievitch, tell me what you think I should do.

Why don't you visit me anymore? Let me see you now and then. These days, the only time I catch a glimpse of you is at Mass on Sundays. Why are you keeping your distance? Have you stopped caring for me? I feel so alone without you, especially in the evenings when the day fades into twilight.

When Thedora is out, I sit here and think about the past—its happiness and its pain. Everything comes back to me so vividly, as if it's happening all over again. I see familiar faces that feel so real, like they're here in the room with me. Most of all, I see my mother. Oh, the dreams I have!

I feel my health failing me, Makar Alexievitch. This morning when I got out of bed, I was so weak that I vomited. I can't shake the feeling that my end is near. Who will bury me when I'm gone? Who will visit my grave or mourn for me? And if I take that job, I might even die in a strange house, among strangers, far from anyone I know. How sad life can be!

Why do you send me treats like candy? Where do you find the money for such things? Please, save your money. You need it.

Thedora sold a carpet I made and got fifty roubles for it—much more than I expected. I'll give her three roubles as a thank-you and use the rest to buy a simple, warm dress. I'm also planning to make a waistcoat for you. I'll sew it myself from good fabric.

Thedora also brought me a book, The Stories of Bielkin, which I can send you if you'd like to read it. Just don't damage it or keep it too long—it doesn't belong to me. It's by Pushkin. Two years ago, I read those stories with my mother, and it hurts too much to read them again.

If you have any books, please let me borrow them—but not the ones from Rataziaev. I'm sure he'll give you one of his own works once it's published, but I honestly can't understand how you enjoy his writing. To me, it's just nonsense!

I'm sorry for writing so much. When I'm sad, I find it helps to talk—or in this case, to write. It's like medicine for me, easing the heaviness in my heart.

Goodbye for now, my dear friend.

Your own,

B.D.

June 28th.

My dearest Barbara Alexievna,

Don't let yourself feel so down! Really, my dear, you should be ashamed to let such gloomy thoughts creep into your mind. Believe me, you are perfectly fine—truly, you are, my love. You look radiant, even blooming. Yes, your face may be a little pale, but you're still as lovely as ever. Forget about dreams and dark thoughts—they're nothing but nonsense. Honestly, you need to brush them aside and not dwell on them.

Why do I feel so well all the time? Why do I sleep peacefully and stay healthy? Look at me! I live well, I rest soundly, and I'm strong enough to handle the younger fellows at work. You should take a cue from me, my dear. Stop worrying so much and cheer up. I know how easily your thoughts can wander, how quickly your imagination can take over, but please, for my sake, don't let it.

You ask me if you should take that position? Absolutely not! No, no, no! How could you even consider such a thing? I won't let you go. If it came to it, I'd sell my coat and walk the streets in my shirt sleeves before letting you want for anything. But I know you, Barbara. This is just a trick—a scheme. Likely, Thedora is behind it all. That woman seems to be able to talk you into anything. Don't listen to her. You know as much as she does, if not more. She's just a foolish, quarrelsome old woman. No, you mustn't take this step. What would I do if you left? What would become of me?

You have everything you need here. I couldn't be happier being close to you, and you love me, too. You can live quietly, just as you like. Read, sew, or both—it's up to you. Just don't leave me. Imagine how empty things would feel if you were gone. I send you books, and we'll go for walks together. Come now, Barbara! Think it over and set aside these silly notions.

As soon as I can, I'll come to see you, and we'll talk it all over. This simply won't do, my love. It's not right. True, I know I'm not an educated man and haven't had much schooling. Maybe I admire Rataziaev too much, but he's my friend, and I have to stand up for him. He's a brilliant writer. I'll never agree with you about his works. Perhaps you read them when you were feeling down or upset with Thedora? Try reading them when you're in a good mood, with a bonbon or two at hand. That's the best way to enjoy Rataziaev.

Well, I must go to work now. Be cheerful, and may God watch over you.

Your faithful friend,

Makar Dievushkin

P.S. Thank you so much for the book! I'll read this volume of Pushkin and bring it with me when I visit tonight.

My dear Makar Alexievitch,

No, no, my friend—I must not stay here near you any longer. I've thought it over carefully and decided it would be wrong to turn down such a good position. At least it would give me a steady income, and I could try to earn my employer's approval and perhaps even change my nature if I had to.

Yes, living among strangers will be hard, and I'll have to hide parts of myself, but God will help me through it. I can't stay a recluse forever. Opportunities like this have come before, and I've let them pass.

When I was a little girl in school, I used to come home on Sundays full of energy, dancing and playing. My mother would sometimes scold me, but I didn't care because I was so happy. Yet when Sunday evening came, I felt such sadness knowing I had to return to school. Everything there was so cold and strict. On Mondays, the governesses were irritable and often punished me, making me cry. Still, I kept my tears to myself to avoid being called lazy. Eventually, I adjusted, but it was always hard to say goodbye to the friends I made.

I can't keep living dependent on you—it tortures me to think of it. I see how hard Thedora works, from dawn until late at night, her poor old body aching. And you—ruining yourself for my sake, spending your last kopeck on me. You shouldn't do this, even if you say you'd give up everything for me. I believe in your good heart, but we have to think about the future.

You know how often I'm unwell. I can't work like you do, no matter how much I'd like to. So what can I do? Sit and watch you and Thedora struggle while I contribute nothing? How would that help anyone?

Am I really necessary to you, my dear friend? Have I ever brought you any real good? Though I love you with all my heart and soul, I have nothing else to offer but that love. I can't repay you for your kindness by making a life for us both.

So please, don't try to stop me. Think it over, and let me know what you decide.

Your devoted,

B.D.

July 1st.

My dearest Barbara Alexievna,

Nonsense, nonsense, Barbara! What you're saying is pure nonsense. Stay here, forget these thoughts, and put them out of your mind. None of what you're imagining is true—I can see that myself. Whatever you need here, just ask me for it. You are loved here, and you love in return. We could be happy and content together. What more could you possibly want? Why do you need strangers? You have no idea what strangers are like, but I do.

I've lived with strangers, eaten their bread. There's one in particular I know—he's cruel, Barbara. He's the kind of man who would break your tender heart with his harsh words, reproaches, and scowls. Here, you are safe, like a bird in a nest. If you leave, what will happen to me? What would I, an old man, do without you? You are everything to me—necessary and useful in ways you might not even realize.

Barbara, you make my life better. Even now, just thinking of you lifts my spirits. I write you letters and pour my thoughts into them, and then I receive your kind, detailed replies. I've bought you a wardrobe and a bonnet, haven't I? You only need to ask, and I'll make sure you have whatever you need. How could I get along without you in my old age? Maybe you've never stopped to think about that. I've grown so used to you that I can't imagine life without you. If you left, I'd be lost.

Do you really want me to end up at the Neva River, ready to throw myself in? Do you want me to end up buried in Volkovo Cemetery, with no one but a street beggar to mourn me and the gravediggers tossing dirt over my coffin as they hurry away? How could you wish that for me, Barbara?

I've returned your book, and if you ask my opinion, I'd say it's wonderful. I can't believe I've gone this long without reading anything like it. What have I been doing all my life? I've read so little—only "A Portrait of Man," "The Boy Who Could Play Many Tunes Upon Bells," and "Ivik's Storks." That's it. But now I've read "The Station Overseer" from your book, and it feels like my own life is laid out on the page.

This book captures life so vividly—it's like the characters are alive. As I read, I almost cried when Samson Virin drank himself into misery, mourning his lost daughter, Dunasha. It felt so real, so close to life. You should read it again. It's a book that speaks to the heart and shows us our world like a mirror. Even Theresa and Gorshkov remind me of the characters in it.

You're thinking of leaving, but you need to understand how much harm that could bring—to both of us. What would you do out there? How would you protect yourself from harm? Listen to me, Barbara—stay. Read your book again. It might help you see things more clearly.

Rataziaev says "The Station Overseer" is old-fashioned, that books today come with illustrations and other embellishments. Still, he respects Pushkin, calling him a poet who has honored Russia. So, read the book again and take my advice. It will do you good, and it would make me, an old man, so very happy. The Lord will surely bless you for it.

Your faithful friend,

Makar Dievushkin

My dearest Makar Alexievitch,

Today, Thedora brought me fifteen roubles in silver. You should have seen how happy she was when I gave her three of them! I'm writing this quickly because I'm busy sewing a waistcoat for you. It's buff-colored with a floral pattern. I'm also sending you a book of stories. I've read some of them myself, especially one called "The Cloak."

You've invited me to the theater, but wouldn't that cost too much? We could sit in the gallery, of course, but it's been so long since I last went to the theater that I can't even remember when it was! Still, I worry it might be more than we can afford.

Thedora keeps shaking her head and saying that you're living beyond your means. I've noticed the same thing from all you've spent on me. Be careful, dear friend. I'd hate for trouble to come of it. Thedora even mentioned rumors about you struggling to pay your landlady. That has me very worried.

Now, I must go. I need to handle some other tasks, like changing the ribbons on my bonnet.
P.S. If we do go to the theater, I think I'll wear my new hat and black mantilla. Won't that look lovely?

Yours always,

Barbara

July 7th.

My dearest Barbara Alexievna,

So much for yesterday! Yes, my dear, it seems we've both been caught acting foolishly, as I've become quite infatuated with the actress I told you about. Last night, I listened to her with complete attention, even though, strangely enough, it was practically my first real time seeing her. I had only been to the theater once before. Back then, I lived in close quarters with a group of five young men—a noisy bunch—and one evening, they dragged me along to the theater. Though I kept to myself and avoided joining in their antics, I went with them just to keep them company.

How they talked about this actress! Every night when the theater was open, the whole group (they always seemed to have enough money) would head straight to the theater, climb up to the gallery, clap their hands wildly, and call for encores from the actress they adored. They practically worshiped her. Even after we got home, they wouldn't stop talking about her all night long, calling her "their Glasha" and "the canary of their hearts." Being as young as they were, they pulled me into their obsession.

Imagine what I must have looked like up there with them in the fourth-tier gallery! I barely got to see anything more than a sliver of the curtain. Mostly, I just listened. She had such a beautiful voice, rich and smooth, like a nightingale. We all clapped as hard as we could and shouted until we nearly got thrown out.

The first time, I left the theater walking in a daze, with only a single rouble left in my pocket and ten whole days to go until my next payday. But guess what, my dear? The very next morning, before work, I went to a French perfumery and spent my last bit of money on eau de cologne and scented soap! Why did I do it? I have no idea.

That same day, I skipped lunch and spent all my time wandering back and forth beneath her apartment windows. She lived in a fourth-floor flat on Nevski Prospect. After a short rest at home, I returned to her street to start pacing beneath her windows again.

For a month and a half, I kept this up, following her wherever I could. Sometimes, I even hired cabs just so I could get out and walk near her place. Eventually, I completely ruined myself and fell into debt. That was when I finally grew tired of the whole pursuit.

So, you see, Barbara, just how far an actress can lead an otherwise decent man astray. Back then, I was young—oh, so very young.

M. D.

July 8th.

My dearest Barbara Alexievna,

I am returning the book you sent me on the 6th along with this letter to explain myself. What a pity, my dear, that you've put me in this situation! Our lives are determined by the Almighty according to what we deserve. Some people are meant to lead—given the life of a general or a counselor—while others are assigned a life of quiet toil and hardship. Each person's path is matched to their abilities, decided by God Himself.

I've spent thirty years in public service, fulfilling my duties without fault. I've lived modestly and avoided any improper behavior. Yes, I admit I've had my shortcomings, as everyone does, but I've also had my virtues. My superiors respect me, even if they've never shown me special favor, and even his Excellency has found no fault with me. My handwriting is clear, neither too fancy nor too plain, and it's legible enough for anyone to read. Only Ivan Prokofievitch writes as well as I do in our office.

I've lived like this into old age, with gray hair and no major regrets. Of course, everyone makes small mistakes—you, too, my dear—but I've never committed serious offenses or broken rules. I've never disturbed the peace or brought shame upon myself. Surely, you know this to be true, just as the author of that book should have known better.

Why shouldn't I continue living quietly in my modest corner of the world, causing no trouble, fearing God, and taking care of myself? I only try to make sure my clothes are decent, my shoes are wearable, and I have enough to eat. If I write about myself too much, is it wrong? Should I instead worry about someone else's problems, about whether someone else has tea to drink?

I don't pry into other people's lives or offend anyone. I live my life peacefully, working hard and earning my way. Yet, a man can work tirelessly, earn respect, and still find himself ridiculed for no reason. Sometimes, people just need a moment to feel proud—perhaps by buying a new pair of shoes and enjoying how they look.

I admit, Barbara, that I've indulged in such small joys myself. Yet, it amazes me how some people endure insults without defending themselves. Even Thedor Thedorovitch, who is known to scold and criticize, has his reasons. People humor him and work around him, but even he has a role in the natural order of things. Everyone in society follows a system, taking their place and sometimes venting their frustrations.

Why do I do my job at all? Does my work bring me a new coat or a pair of shoes? No, people read what I write and then ask me to write more. Some people avoid the world entirely, fearing gossip and slander, even if they've done nothing wrong. Others keep their heads down, live a decent life, and die respected but forgotten.

Wouldn't it be better if, instead of being praised after death, such a person received kindness while still alive? If their superiors recognized their worth and rewarded them with a promotion or a raise? That would bring peace and fairness to the workplace.

So, my dear, why did you send me that book? It paints an unrealistic picture of life and of people like me. There's no such official as the one described in its pages. I must protest, Barbara, against such a misrepresentation.

Your humble and devoted servant,

M. D.

July 27th.

My dearest Makar Alexievitch,

Your recent actions and letters have left me deeply shaken and full of doubt. It wasn't until your explanation about Thedora that I began to understand. Why fall into such despair and act so recklessly, Makar Alexievitch? Your words only partly satisfy me. Perhaps I was wrong to insist on accepting a good position when it was offered, especially after my last experience, which was anything but pleasant.

You also say that your love for me led you to withdraw from the world. I cannot describe how much your kindness has meant to me, especially when I learned that the money you were said to have saved in the bank never existed. Instead, you used your entire salary—and even borrowed against it—to help me when you learned of my destitution. When I was ill, you even sold your own clothes.

Hearing this, I don't know how to accept everything you've done for me or what to think of it. Oh, Makar Alexievitch, you should have stopped after your initial acts of kindness, which were born out of sympathy and family love. Instead, you went on to spend money on things that were unnecessary.

You've betrayed our friendship by not being honest with me. Now that I know your last coins were spent on gifts like dresses, sweets, trips to the theater, and books for me, I feel nothing but regret. I weep bitterly over my thoughtlessness in accepting these things without considering how it might affect you.

Recently, I noticed how sad you seemed, and I feared something was wrong. But I could never have imagined this. To think your better judgment could fail you so! What will people think of you? What will they say? How will they treat you now? I valued you for your kind heart, your modesty, and your good sense. But now, you've fallen into a habit I never thought you capable of.

How shocked I was when Thedora told me you'd been found drunk in the street and taken home by the police! It left me utterly speechless, though I had grown worried when I didn't hear from you for four days. Have you thought about what your superiors will say when they discover the truth behind your absence?

You say people are laughing at you, mocking our bond, and making rude comments about me. Please, Makar Alexievitch, pay no attention to them. For God's sake, don't let it trouble you. But the incident with the officers has deeply alarmed me. I've heard rumors but don't know the full story. Please explain it to me.

You say you were afraid to be honest with me because you thought I might stop being your friend. You also say you're in despair because you've spent everything helping me, even borrowing money, and now you're facing trouble with your landlady. But hiding the truth from me was the worst choice you could have made. Now that I know everything, I see how I've brought you so much suffering, and it breaks my heart.

It pains me to think that I've caused you such hardship, bringing calamities into your once quiet, simple life. This realization tortures me more than I can express.

Please, Makar Alexievitch, write to me honestly. Tell me how this all began and what drove you to act this way. Comfort me, if you can. I don't ask this for selfish reasons but out of love and friendship for you. My feelings for you will never fade from my heart.

Goodbye for now. I wait for your reply with great impatience. You've misunderstood me, Makar Alexievitch.

Your friend and devoted companion,

Barbara Dobroselova

July 28th.

My priceless Barbara Alexievna,

What can I say now that everything has passed and we're trying to get back to how things were before? You mentioned being worried about how others view me. Let me assure you, the most important thing to me is my self-respect. That's why, even as I've shared my troubles and mistakes with you, I can tell you with confidence that none of my superiors know about them, nor will they ever know. Because of that, I still hold some degree of respect in their eyes.

The only thing I fear is gossip. While my landlady loves to talk, she didn't say much when I used your ten roubles to partially pay my rent today. As for the others around me, they don't matter much. Since I haven't borrowed money from them, I don't have to worry about their opinions.

Above everything else in the world, I treasure your respect for me. It has been my greatest comfort during this difficult time. Thank God the worst of it has passed, and you no longer see me as selfish or untrustworthy simply because I wasn't honest with you. I cannot bear the thought of losing you, Barbara. I love you dearly, like my own guardian angel.

I've returned to work now and am putting all my effort into my duties. Yesterday, Evstafi Ivanovitch even exchanged a few words with me. Still, I won't hide from you the fact that my debts are weighing heavily on me, and my wardrobe is in poor shape. But these things aren't so important, so please don't let them upset you.

If you can, send me another half-rouble. Though it pains me deeply to ask, knowing that it's you helping me instead of the other way around, it would be a big help. Thedora did well to get those fifteen roubles for you. As for myself, I currently have no way of finding more money—foolish old man that I am—but as soon as I do, I will let you know.

What bothers me the most is the fear of gossip. Goodbye, my little angel. I kiss your hands and beg you to take care of your health. This letter is not as detailed as it could be, but I need to leave for work soon. I want to make up for my past mistakes by dedicating myself to my job. I'll write more tonight, including about what happened with the officers.

Your affectionate and respectful friend,

Makar Dievushkin

July 28th.

Dearest Barbara Alexievna,

It is you who have made a mistake, and it must weigh heavily on your conscience. Your last letter has shocked and confused me so much that, after reflecting deeply, I still believe my actions were right. Of course, I am not talking about my disgraceful behavior—no, not that—but about the fact that I love you, though I know it's unwise of me. You don't fully understand my reasons for loving you, my dear. If you did, you wouldn't say the things you do. I'm convinced it's your mind, not your heart, that is speaking, for I believe your heart feels differently.

As for what happened that night with those officers, I hardly remember it. Please understand that I have been in terrible distress for some time now. For a whole month, I have been hanging by a thread. My situation has been truly miserable. Though I tried to hide my troubles from you, my landlady wouldn't stop yelling and complaining at me. Her shouting wouldn't have mattered much—she could have yelled all she liked—but it was humiliating. Worse, she somehow discovered our connection and began spreading it throughout the household, yelling about it until I felt deafened and had to cover my ears. Yet others didn't stop their ears. They listened and gossiped, and now I don't know what to do.

This wretched situation has driven me to the edge. It started when I heard from Thedora about an unworthy suitor who had visited you and insulted you with an inappropriate proposal. I knew how deeply it must have hurt you because I felt equally insulted. That was when I lost control. Overcome with rage and confusion, I didn't know what to do but was determined to confront this villain. However, I feared offending you. What a terrible, stormy night it was—rain and sleet everywhere! Eventually, I found myself too unsteady to stand.

That's when Emelia Ilyitch appeared. He used to work as a government clerk but lost his position some time ago. Why he was there at that moment, I have no idea, but I ended up going with him. Surely, it won't bring you any joy to read about your friend's troubles, sorrows, and temptations.

On the third evening, Emelia encouraged me to confront the officer. I had already learned his address from our building attendant and had even followed him home once after seeing him play cards here. Looking back, I realize this was wrong, but I was overwhelmed when I heard what he had been saying about me.

I don't remember exactly what happened next. There were several officers there, including the one I sought. Or maybe I saw double—I can't be sure. I only know that I said a lot in my fury, though I can't recall my words. They ended up throwing me out and shoving me down the stairs. You already know how I got home. That's all I can tell you.

Later, I blamed myself and felt my pride take a fall. However, no one knows about this except you, so it doesn't matter. Perhaps the incident wasn't as bad as you imagine. I do know that, last year, one of our lodgers, Aksenti Osipovitch, handled a similar matter with dignity. He called Peter Petrovitch into his room, had a private conversation (I watched through a crack in the wall), and settled things as a gentleman would. Afterward, they acted as if nothing had happened.

In my case, though, I didn't handle things with such calm. I admit I've made a grave mistake, but I believe it was fate. We cannot escape fate, my dear.

Here is a detailed explanation of my misfortunes and sorrows, written for you to read whenever it's convenient. I am not feeling well, my love, and my spirits are low, but I send you this letter as a sign of my love, devotion, and respect.

Your humble servant,

Makar Dievushkin

July 29th.

My Dearest Makar Alexievitch,

I have read your two letters, and they have left me with a heavy heart. Listen, my dear friend—you seem to avoid mentioning certain things and only write about part of your troubles. Could it be that your letters are written under some kind of mental strain?

Please, for the love of God, come and see me. Come today, straight from the office, and have dinner with us as you've done before. I have no idea how you're living now or what sort of arrangement you've made with your landlady because you've left those details out. It seems like you've purposely avoided talking about them.

Come to me today without fail. It would be much better if you always had your meals here. Thedora is an excellent cook.

Goodbye for now, my dear friend. I'm waiting for you.

Your own,

Barbara Dobroselova

August 1st.

My Dearest Barbara Alexievna,

Thank God you have found a way to repay my kindness. I believe in you and the goodness of your heart, so I won't blame you for anything. But please, don't criticize me for spending too much during the later years of my life. Was it really such a terrible thing to do? Even if you think it was, you must know how much it pains me to hear those words from you. Don't be upset with me for saying this, for my heart feels weak. Poor people often have strange thoughts—that's just how it is. I've experienced it myself.

Poor people are always on edge. They can't see the world the way others do. Instead, they're always watching, always listening, always wondering what others are saying about them. Do people think they look shabby? Do they pity them or judge them? Poor people are seen as less than nothing and never earn anyone's respect. Writers may try to tell their stories, but nothing ever changes. Why? Because the poor are forced to live with their hearts exposed, and nothing about them is private. Even their self-respect is taken away.

The other day, Emelia told me how, when he had to collect donations, people wouldn't give a single coin without official approval. They thought a poor man couldn't be trusted with their money. That's the way charity works these days—perhaps it's always been that way. People either don't know how to help, or they're just too clever about it.

The poor man learns these things through experience. He watches as a wealthy man walks into a restaurant, orders whatever he wants, and enjoys a fine meal, while the poor man has nothing but thin gruel. There are busybodies who go around looking for someone whose boots are falling apart or whose hair is unkempt, just to gossip about them. Why does it matter if my hair needs cutting? The poor man feels shame as deeply as a young girl would if forced to undress in public. It's painful and humiliating.

Today at work, I sat among my colleagues feeling like a miserable fool. I could barely look them in the eye. My clothes were in such bad shape—my toes poking out of my boots, my buttons barely holding on. I felt so embarrassed, especially when Stepan Karlovitch suddenly said, "Ah, poor Makar Alexievitch," and then stopped himself. I knew what he meant, and I blushed so hard even my bald spot must have turned red.

It's nothing, really, but it weighs on my mind. What do they know about me? I pray they know nothing, though I suspect someone has been talking. Perhaps it's Rataziaev—he probably told someone in his department, and the gossip spread to mine. I've even seen people pointing at you through the window, and when I came to visit you, the whole group was staring at me. The landlady called you rude names, too.

And that's not the worst of it. Rataziaev has hinted that he might use us in one of his stories, making us the subjects of his satire. I don't know what to do about it. It's clear we've made mistakes, and for that, I feel regret.

You mentioned sending me a book to distract me. What kind of book could possibly help now? Most books are nonsense, written for idle people with nothing better to do. Even Shakespeare—people praise him endlessly, but I say his works are nothing more than silly plays.

Yours always,

Makar Dievushkin

August 2nd.

My Dearest Makar Alexievitch,

Please don't worry yourself. God will help everything work out in the end. Thedora has managed to find plenty of work for both of us, and we've already started on it with determination. Maybe this will help us get back on track. Thedora thinks my recent troubles are somehow tied to Anna Thedorovna, but I don't really care—I feel unusually cheerful today.

So, you're thinking about borrowing more money? May God protect you, because if you do, you'll surely find yourself in ruin when it's time to pay it back! It would be much better if you came to live with us for a while. Yes, come stay here, and don't worry about what your landlady might say. As for the rest of your so-called enemies or those who wish you harm, I'm sure you're just letting your imagination get the better of you.

By the way, I've noticed that your writing style changes a lot from one letter to the next. Goodbye for now. I'm looking forward to seeing you soon. I'm waiting for you with impatience.

Yours always,

B.D.

August 3rd.

My dearest Barbara Alexievna,

I'm writing to tell you, my dear, that my hopes have risen again. But, my little one, do you really mean it when you say I shouldn't borrow any more money? How could I manage without it? Things would go badly for both of us if I stopped borrowing. You're not well, and because of that, I must keep borrowing. There's no other way.

I've been moved to sit next to a man named Emelia Ivanovitch at work. He's not the Emelia you know but another man, also a privy councillor and one of the oldest employees in our department, like me. He's a decent, quiet fellow, though his gruff appearance makes him seem like a bear. He works hard and has an oddly English-style handwriting—actually worse than mine! Even though we've never been close, we've always been polite, exchanging greetings and occasionally borrowing each other's penknife.

Today, Emelia asked me, "Makar Alexievitch, why do you look so thoughtful?" I could tell he meant well, so I told him a little about my troubles—not everything, of course, just a few details about my financial situation. He suggested I borrow money from Peter Petrovitch, who lends money at reasonable interest rates. Hearing this, I felt a spark of hope. If I could get a loan from him, I could pay off my landlady, help you, and get away from the people who mock me.

So, summoning my courage, I approached Peter Petrovitch. I was trembling inside, but I decided to give it a try. He was busy talking to someone else when I pulled at his sleeve and explained my situation. At first, he didn't understand what I was asking. When I repeated my request for a thirty-rouble loan, he laughed and went back to his work without responding.

I tried again, explaining that although I had no collateral, I would use my future salary to repay him. But even then, he barely acknowledged me. When he was called away and returned, he simply mended his pen, ignoring me. Finally, I gave up and left.

They're all good people, Barbara, but so proud. What can someone like me do around them? Still, I wanted to tell you everything. Emelia, kind soul that he is, encouraged me. He even promised to recommend me to a friend of his who lends money. This friend lives on Viborskaia Street, and Emelia is confident he'll help. So tomorrow, I plan to visit this gentleman.

What do you think of this, my dear? I have to try—my landlady is threatening to evict me, and I can't afford food. My boots are falling apart, with no buttons left, and I don't own another pair. Can you imagine anyone looking shabbier in a government office? It's terrible, Barbara—simply terrible!

Makar Dievushkin

August 4th.

My dearest Makar Alexievitch,

Please, I beg you, try to borrow some money as soon as you can. I wouldn't ask you for this if I weren't in such a difficult situation. Thedora and I can no longer stay in our current lodgings because we've faced so much unpleasantness. You can't imagine how upset and worried I am.

This morning, an older man, nearly elderly, came to visit us. His chest was covered in medals. I was very surprised and asked what he wanted, as Thedora was out shopping at the time. Instead of answering, he started questioning me about my life and work. Before I could even reply, he introduced himself as the uncle of the officer you mentioned before. He said he was angry with his nephew for behaving badly, especially for spreading rumors about me, and that he wanted to protect me from his nephew's insolence.

He told me to stay away from young men like his nephew and said he felt like a father to me and would gladly help in any way he could. His words confused me, but I didn't thank him much. Then, without warning, he grabbed my hand and, tapping my cheek, said I was very pretty and that he liked the dimples in my face. God only knows what he meant! Then he even tried to kiss me, saying it was harmless since he was an old man.

Thankfully, at that moment, Thedora returned. Embarrassed, the man repeated how much he respected my modesty and virtue and said he wanted to get to know me better. He even tried to give Thedora money under some excuse, but of course, she refused. Before leaving, he said he would come back with a pair of earrings for me and that I should change my lodgings. He claimed to know of a great flat that would cost me nothing and kept praising my good sense and purity. He also mentioned that Anna Thedorovna had sent him and that she planned to visit me herself soon.

It was then I understood everything. I can hardly remember what I did next, as I've never been in such a situation before, but I believe I completely lost my temper. Thedora and I made the old man leave, and she nearly threw him out herself. We're certain this is all Anna Thedorovna's doing. How else would that man have known about us?

Now, Makar Alexievitch, I have no choice but to turn to you for help. Please, for the love of God, don't leave me in this terrible situation. I have no money to leave these lodgings, but I absolutely cannot stay here any longer. Thedora agrees that we need at least twenty-five roubles. I promise to repay you from what I earn through my work. Thedora will also help me find more work so that even if there's heavy interest on the loan, you won't have to bear the burden. I'll give you everything I have if only you'll continue to help me.

I hate to trouble you when I know you're struggling too, but I have no one else to turn to. You're my only hope. Please think of me, and may God guide you in this.

Yours,

B.D.

August 4th.

My beloved Barbara Alexievna,

These unexpected misfortunes have struck me hard, and the strange series of calamities we're facing has completely crushed my spirit. It feels as though these vile gossips and pestilent old men are not content with tormenting you—they seem intent on dragging me down as well. And they're succeeding. I assure you, they are. Yet I swear to you, I would rather die than fail to help you. If I can't help you, I will die. But for me to help you, my dear, you must flee from this wretched place. You must leave this nest where these cruel owls, these predators, are trying to destroy you.

How deeply distressed I feel, my dearest! And yet, you are so cruel to yourself. Even as you endure pain and humiliation, even as your spirit suffers terribly, you tell me that it grieves you to trouble me. You even say that you'll work off your debt with your own hands. You, with your delicate health, propose to ruin yourself to ease my financial burdens! My dear, stop and think about what you're saying. Why should you exhaust yourself with sewing and overwork? Why torment your mind with anxiety, strain your beautiful eyes, and sacrifice your health? Why should you do this?

Oh, little Barbara, sweet Barbara! Don't you see that I can never be any real good to you? Never, no matter how much I might want to be. I know this, but even so, I will find a way to help you. I will overcome every obstacle. I will take on extra work, copy manuscripts for writers, and even approach them personally to demand they employ me. I will apply myself with such diligence that they will see I am a skilled copyist, and skilled copyists are always needed. You will not have to wear yourself out; I won't allow it. I will not let you carry out this terrible plan of yours.

Yes, my angel, I will borrow money. I'd rather die than fail to do so. Just tell me that you don't mind if I face heavy interest, and I'll endure it. I won't hesitate; I won't shrink back. To begin with, I'll try to borrow forty roubles. It's not much, is it, Barbara? But do you think anyone will trust me with that sum right away? Do I look like the sort of man who inspires confidence at first sight? Does my appearance give anyone a favorable impression? You know it doesn't. I've never been able to make a good impression on anyone. What do you think?

Honestly, just imagining the difficulties ahead makes me feel sick at heart. But if I manage to get forty roubles, I'll set aside twenty-five for you, two for my landlady, and the rest for my own needs. I know I should give the landlady more, but you must understand my situation. It's all I can spare. Let's leave it at that.

Out of the remaining roubles, one will go toward buying a new pair of shoes. I'm not sure my current ones will even hold up until tomorrow when I need to go to the office. I also need a new neck scarf because my old one has been worn out for over a year. Thankfully, you've promised to turn your old apron into both a scarf and a shirt-front for me, so I'll manage without buying a new one. That leaves buttons. Barbara, you know I can't go without buttons. My clothing is falling apart—every hem is frayed. I shudder to think that one day his Excellency might notice my untidiness. What would he say? What wouldn't he say? Yet I'll never hear his words because I'll have died of shame on the spot.

Ah, my darling, my poor angel! When all my necessities are taken care of, I'll have about three roubles left. I'll spend part of that on half a pound of tobacco. It's been nine days since I last smoked my pipe, and I can't do without it. I confess this to you now because my conscience won't let me hide it. I feel terrible that while you deprive yourself of everything, I seek small comforts.

To be honest, I'm in the worst situation I've ever known. My landlady mocks me, no one respects me, and my debts are crushing. Even at the office, where I've never felt particularly welcome, no one speaks to me anymore. But I keep all of this hidden. I hide everything, even my own person, as much as I can. If I didn't have to go to the office every day and face my colleagues, I'd disappear entirely. Yet, writing to you about these troubles strengthens my spirit.

We must not dwell on these hardships, my dear Barbara, or let them break our resolve. I'm only writing about them to warn you not to dwell on such thoughts yourself. Do not torture yourself with dark imaginings. But, oh God, what will become of us?

Stay where you are until I can come to you. Once I'm with you, I won't return here. I'll simply vanish. For now, I must end this letter and go shave. It's remarkable how much shaving can improve one's sense of decency. One prayer to God, and then I'll be on my way.

M. Dievushkin

August 5th.

Dearest Makar Alexievitch,

You must not despair, my dear friend. Push away this gloom and melancholy. I am sending you thirty kopecks in silver. I wish it could be more, but it is all I have to give right now. Use it to buy whatever you most urgently need until tomorrow. As for me, I have almost nothing left, and I do not know what I am going to do. Isn't it terrible, Makar Alexievitch? Yet even in this dire situation, you must not give in to despair. There is no use in letting sorrow overwhelm us.

Thedora believes it might not be a bad idea for us to remain in this tenement for now. She says that if we leave, suspicions might arise, and our enemies might decide to come after us. She could be right. But I can't help feeling that staying here might not be the best choice either. If only I weren't so weighed down with sadness, I could explain my reasons more clearly.

Oh, Makar Alexievitch, what a strange and sensitive man you are! You let things affect you so deeply that you hardly know what it means to be happy. I have read your letters carefully, and each one shows me just how much you worry about me. Yet in all your worrying and fretting, you never seem to think of yourself. Every word tells me of your kind and selfless heart, but I fear that your kindness is too great—it's overwhelming.

Allow me to give you a bit of friendly advice, Makar Alexievitch. I am deeply grateful to you—truly, I am—for all that you have done for me. Your goodness humbles me, and I feel it deeply. But it pains me to see that, despite all your own troubles (troubles for which I feel I have been an unintentional cause), you live entirely for me. Your every thought is for my happiness, my sorrows, my wellbeing. You think only of me, to the point where you forget yourself entirely.

If you continue to take someone else's troubles so deeply to heart, if you continue to bear my burdens as if they were your own, it is no wonder that you are unhappy. Today, when you came to see me after your office work was done, I could scarcely look into your eyes. You seemed so pale, so worn out, and your face looked thinner than ever. I could see how afraid you were—afraid to tell me that you hadn't been able to borrow the money, afraid to upset or worry me. And yet, when you saw that I managed to smile, even a little, I could sense the weight lifting from your heart.

Oh, Makar Alexievitch, please do not let this sadness consume you. Do not give in to despair. You must trust that better days are coming. I implore you to give yourself over to hope, to rely on your better judgment. Believe me, it won't be long before things start to turn around for us. But if you continue to let my sorrows drag you down, you will only spoil your own life, and I cannot bear to see that happen.

So, my dear friend, take care of yourself. Do not let your heart be so heavy. And most importantly, do not be overly anxious about me. Goodbye for now, Makar Alexievitch. I will be thinking of you always.

B. D.

August 5th.

My darling little Barbara,

It brings me such relief to hear from you, to feel the warmth of your words despite the hardships we both endure. You reassure me with your kindness, telling me that my failure to secure money does not trouble you, and for that, I am deeply grateful. Your understanding lightens my heavy heart. It brings me joy to know that you do not plan to abandon your current lodgings, that you will not leave me in spirit, even if the world seems intent on conspiring against us. Your letter has filled me with a sense of hope and a recognition of your boundless compassion, which I can only humbly acknowledge. How good it feels to know that you care for my feelings, that you love me enough to be so concerned. I do not say this out of pride but out of gratitude.

You bid me not to lose heart, and I am trying, dearest. I am trying for your sake. Today, as I look at the pair of shoes I shall wear to the office tomorrow, I feel a strange sense of resolve. It is true that dwelling too much on one's troubles can unravel a person completely. What sustains me is knowing that my grief, my struggles, are not for myself but for you. I could endure walking through the bitter cold without an overcoat or boots if it were only my pride at stake. I am a simple man with few needs. But what would people say? What would those envious, judgmental voices whisper if they saw me without proper clothing? It is for others' eyes that one must maintain appearances, not for oneself. Without an overcoat, my name and reputation would be tarnished.

Yet, let me tell you about my day. It has been one of agony, a torment that feels as though it has stretched across years. This morning, I set out early, before the office opened, to meet the man of whom I had spoken. Rain and sleet poured down as I wrapped myself tightly in my greatcoat. I whispered prayers as I walked, asking for forgiveness for my sins and hoping for some divine intervention. Passing a church, I crossed myself and reminded myself of my unworthiness before God. I tried to shut out the world and focus inward, not daring to notice the dreariness of the streets or the careworn faces of those around me.

Near the Voskresenski Bridge, exhaustion began to weigh on me. My feet ached, and each step became a struggle. Then I saw a colleague from the office, Ermolaev, who stopped to stare at me as though asking for something I could not give. His gaze unsettled me, and I hurried on. My thoughts were scattered, my appearance shabby, and shame burned in my chest. Finally, I saw the house—a yellow, gabled building that looked as though it might belong to the Monsieur Markov Emelia Ivanovitch had mentioned.

Approaching the gate, I felt an overwhelming dread. A watchman muttered unkindly when I asked for directions, and my unease deepened. Three times I passed the house before summoning the courage to enter. Just as I reached the door, a large, ragged dog lunged at me, barking furiously and nearly making me lose my nerve. These little moments, so trivial in the grand scheme of things, nearly crushed me.

Inside, I stumbled immediately into disaster, knocking over an old woman's milk pail and spilling its contents everywhere. Her angry words stung as I tried to explain myself. The mistress of the house appeared—a stern, mean-looking woman—and listened to my awkward request to speak with Monsieur Markov. She called her daughter to fetch him, and I was shown into a room filled with portraits of generals and the faint scent of balsam.

As I waited, doubt consumed me. I wanted to flee, to return another day when the weather might be kinder, or my nerves steadier.

But before I could act on this impulse, Markov entered. His appearance—a shabby dressing gown and a suspicious gaze—did not inspire confidence. I stumbled through my request, explaining my dire need for forty roubles. His response was a firm refusal. "I have no money," he said, dismissing me with cold indifference. My heart sank as I repeated my plea, but he only grew more distant.

Leaving the house, I felt utterly defeated. The cold bit through me as I made my way to the office, arriving late and disheveled. The porter, Sniegirev, refused to let me use the Government brush to clean myself up, mocking my appearance instead. It is these small humiliations, Barbara, that weigh on me most. They are what truly break my spirit.

Yet, reading your letters today brought me a bittersweet comfort. They are a reminder of your steadfast kindness and our shared struggles. My golden days may be behind me, but your words give me strength to face another day.

Goodbye, my dearest Barbara. May the Lord watch over you and keep you safe. Soon, I will come to see you. I promise I will not fail to come.

M. Dievushkin

August 11th.

O Barbara Alexievna,

I am ruined—utterly ruined! We are both lost, you and I, beyond any hope of redemption. Everything has crumbled—my reputation, my dignity, my very sense of self. All that I once had in this world is gone, and you are caught in this same calamity alongside me. Never shall we regain what we have lost. I have dragged you into this despair, my dear. I am the cause, the one who has brought us both to this terrible state.

Everywhere I go, people mock me. They laugh openly and scorn me without hesitation. Even my landlady has joined in. Today she subjected me to a tirade of insults so piercing, so degrading, that I felt reduced to nothing more than the dirt on her doorstep. She shouted at me as though I were a common criminal, as though my very presence defiled her home. And that was not the worst of it.

Last night, while I was at Rataziaev's rooms, one of his friends found a note that I had written to you. It had fallen from my pocket, and they seized upon it as though it were a great prize. Without a shred of decency, they read it aloud. How they laughed, Barbara! How they mocked every word, every sentiment! They derided us both—you and I—like a pack of jackals. I could not stand it. I confronted Rataziaev, accusing him of betraying me, of breaking faith. But he only laughed and turned my words back on me. He accused me of betrayal instead, claiming that I had been indulging in secret affairs. "You've kept your little romances well hidden, haven't you, Mr. Lovelace?" he said. And now, everywhere I go, I am called by that name—"Lovelace." They know everything, Barbara. Everything about us, about you, about me, about our lives. Our private matters have become a source of their amusement.

Even at home, I cannot escape the humiliation. Today, when I asked Phaldoni to fetch something for me from the bakeshop, he flatly refused. "It's not my job," he said. I told him that he must go, but he replied, "Why should I? You haven't paid my mistress what you owe her, so I don't have to run your errands." Can you imagine, Barbara, the audacity of a mere servant speaking to me this way? In my anger, I called him a fool, but he only fired back with more insults. "You dare call me drunk?" he said. "Perhaps you should sober up yourself! Everyone knows you were out drinking the other day with some woman, spending two grivenniks on who knows what."

To hear such words from him, from anyone—it is more than I can bear. My life has become a wretched spectacle, a public humiliation. I feel as though I have been proclaimed a disgrace for all to see. I am worse off than a vagabond without a passport, wandering with no place to call home. How quickly these misfortunes have descended upon me, one after another, like waves crashing down with relentless force.

I am undone, Barbara. Completely undone. There is no escape from this shame, no way to recover the life I have lost. I am lost, my dearest. Lost forever.

M. D.

August 13th.

My dear Makar Alexievitch,

It seems like trouble keeps piling up one after another, and I hardly know what to do anymore. But no matter how difficult things might be for you, I'm afraid you can't look to me for much help. Just today, I burned my left hand with the iron! At the same moment, I dropped it, ruined my work, and hurt myself in the process. Now I can't even work properly. On top of that, Thedora has been unwell for the past three days. The worry is becoming unbearable.

Still, I am sending you thirty kopecks. It's almost the last bit of money I have left, but I wanted to give you something since I know how much you're struggling. I only wish I could do more to help you in your time of need. This situation is so frustrating—it makes me want to cry.

Goodbye for now, my dear friend. If you could come to see me today, it would bring me so much comfort.

B. D.

August 14th.

What is wrong with you, Makar Alexievitch? Have you lost your fear of God? You are not only driving me to despair but also destroying yourself with this constant worry about your reputation. Everyone knows you as a man of honor, dignity, and self-respect, yet you act as though you are constantly ashamed of yourself! Shouldn't you have more regard for your years? It seems the fear of God has left you entirely.

Thedora has told you that I can no longer help you—it's simply beyond my ability. Look at the situation you've put me in! Do you think it means nothing to me to see you behaving this way? Do you think I haven't suffered because of it? I can't even walk down the stairs here without being stared at, pointed at, or spoken about in the most horrible way. People are saying things like, "She's tied to a drunkard!" Imagine what it's like to hear such things! And when you are brought home in such a state, people mockingly say, "There goes that tchinovnik." Is that how you intend to get my help? I swear, I can't stay here any longer. I must leave this place and find work as a cook or a laundress—it's impossible to go on like this.

I wrote to you long ago, asking you to come and see me, but you haven't come. Do my tears and prayers mean nothing to you, Makar Alexievitch? Where did you even find the money for your drinking? For God's sake, take better care of yourself, or you will ruin everything. It's so shameful—so unbearable to think of. I heard that the landlady wouldn't let you in last night and that you spent the night on the doorstep. Yes, I know all about it. If only you could understand how much it hurt me to hear that news!

Please, Makar Alexievitch, come and see me. Let us be happy

together again. We can read together and talk about the old days. Thedora can tell you stories of her pilgrimages from years ago. For the love of God, don't destroy yourself and me along with you. I live only for you. It's for your sake that I'm still here. Be strong again. Be the better version of yourself—the one who can face hardships without giving up. Remember, poverty is not a crime; it's nothing to be ashamed of. Why should we despair? These troubles won't last forever, and God will help us through them. But you must be brave.

I'm sending you two grivenniks to buy some tobacco or whatever you might need, but please don't waste it. Spend it wisely. And please, come and see me soon. Don't feel ashamed to face me, as you did before—there's no need for that. Just come with true repentance and faith in God, who watches over everything and makes things right in the end.

B. D.

August 19th.

My dearest Barbara Alexievna,

Yes, I am ashamed to face you, my dear—I truly am. But at the same time, what's the big deal? Why can't we just move past this and find happiness again? Why should I be upset about my worn-out boots and the soles of my feet showing through? A sole is just a sole—a plain, dirty piece of leather, nothing more. And honestly, shoes are not that important either. The wise Greeks used to walk barefoot, so why should we fuss over such things? Still, I can't understand why I must be insulted and looked down upon because of them.

Please tell Thedora that she is an irritating, tiresome old woman who talks far too much and often says foolish things. As for my grey hairs, you are mistaken about that. I'm not nearly as old as you make me out to be.

Emelia sends his regards to you. You wrote that you are feeling very upset and have been crying. Well, I am also upset and have been crying too. But let's not dwell on that. I wish you nothing but good health and happiness, just as I am trying to stay well and happy myself, as long as I can remain your friend.

Makar Dievushkin

August 21st.

My dear and kind Barbara Alexievna,

I know that I am at fault, and I feel deeply ashamed. I know I've done wrong, but it feels like nothing I do now can make up for it. Even before my mistake, I felt this way—trapped in despair and weighed down by my own shortcomings. My darling, I am not cruel, and I would never intentionally cause you pain. To hurt your gentle heart would be like a tiger attacking a lamb, and I am no tiger. My heart is soft, and you know that I would never willingly harm you. Yet, here I am, full of guilt, though I don't fully understand what I've done wrong. It's a mystery to me.

When you sent me those thirty kopecks, followed by two grivenniks, my heart sank. I couldn't bear to think of you sending me money when you had burned your hand and were likely going hungry yourself. And then, you told me to use that money to buy tobacco! How could I take it? How could I steal from you, an orphan, like some heartless thief? It broke me, dearest. It made me feel even more useless and unworthy, as though I were less than the sole of my own shoe. I started to believe it was ridiculous for me to even try to improve myself, that I was nothing but a disgrace.

Once a person loses their self-respect, it's hard to stop the downward spiral. It's like fate takes over, and they can't pull themselves back up. That evening, I only stepped outside for some fresh air, but one thing led to another. The cold weather, the dreariness of it all— and then, I ran into Emelia.

Emelia had spent everything he had. He hadn't eaten in two days and couldn't even pawn his belongings because the pawnbrokers wouldn't accept them. I didn't help him out of any real friendship, but out of pity for a fellow human being. That's how it happened, my dear. As we talked, he mentioned you, and we both ended up in tears. He's a man with a kind heart, even if his situation is miserable.

Dearest, you must understand that I think of you always. From the moment I met you, you changed my life. Before you came along, I was lonely. It felt like I wasn't even living, just existing. My colleagues used to mock me, saying I was useless, and over time, I started to believe them. I disliked myself because they disliked me.

But then you entered my life. You brought light into my darkness, and you gave me hope. You made me feel like I was worth something, like I wasn't as hopeless as I had thought. For the first time, I saw that I wasn't worse than anyone else. I may not be polished or brilliant, but I realized that my thoughts and feelings were just as valid as those of any other person.

Now, though, it feels like fate is against me again. Misfortune has beaten me down, and I've lost my strength. I've let myself fall back into that old despair, forgetting my own worth. This is my confession to you, my dear. Please don't ask me any more about it—I can't bear it. My heart is heavy, and life feels unbearably hard and bitter.

With all my respect and love, I remain your faithful friend,

Makar Dievushkin

September 3rd.

My dear Makar Alexievitch,

The reason I could not finish my last letter was that writing has become so difficult for me. There are moments when I am grateful to be alone, to grieve and reflect without anyone else to share my sorrow. These moments are becoming more frequent. When I think about my past, I find it both mysterious and strangely captivating, so much so that I can lose myself in those memories for hours. During these times, I forget everything around me, including the reality of my present life. Every impression I encounter now—whether good or bad—seems to bring back memories of something similar from long ago.

My childhood, my golden years, feels particularly vivid in these moments. Yet, these memories leave me feeling drained and sad. They weaken me and exhaust my imagination, making my already fragile health even worse.

Today, though, it is a beautiful morning. The air is fresh and clear, and there isn't a single cloud in the sky. Days like this are so rare in autumn, and I can't help but feel a little uplifted. Still, it's strange to think how quickly the season has changed. I used to love autumn when I was a child. How well I remember those autumn evenings by the pond near our house, at the foot of the hill! The water was so still, its surface smooth and clear like glass.

On quiet evenings, the pond would be perfectly calm. The trees on its banks stood silent, their leaves unmoving. Everything felt so fresh and peaceful, though there was a certain chill in the air. Dew would settle on the grass, and the lights of the nearby huts would flicker in the distance. The cattle would slowly make their way home, and I would slip outside to stand by the pond and lose myself in its beauty.

Sometimes, fishermen would light small fires on the water's edge, and their glow would reflect across the surface. The sky above would be a cool shade of blue, fading into fiery streaks of orange and red near the horizon as the sun set. And when the moon rose, its light would mingle with the faint sounds of the night—a bird startled from its perch, a bulrush brushing against its neighbors, or the soft splash of a fish breaking the surface.

A thin mist would settle over the water, and though the darkness of night seemed to stretch endlessly into the distance, everything close by stood out sharply: the banks, the boats, and the little islands. I remember the way a stray branch or a piece of driftwood would float among the reeds, while a lone gull might suddenly appear, dive into the water, and vanish into the mist again. How deeply I loved those moments! They felt so good, so pure, even though I was just a child then, too young to understand the world fully.

Autumn always had a special charm for me, especially late autumn. By then, the fields would be harvested, the hard work of the season finished, and the village would begin to settle into quiet evenings. Everything seemed mysterious. The sky would be heavy with clouds, and fallen leaves would cover the paths along the edges of the dark, bare forest.

I remember being out late, separated from my companions, and feeling the strange fear that comes with being alone in the woods. The wind would moan and howl, shaking the leafless branches, while flocks of birds flew overhead, their cries filling the air. It was as though the forest itself whispered, urging me to hurry home. I would run as fast as I could, trembling with fear, until I reached the safety of our warm house.

Inside, everything felt alive and comforting. We children would gather around the fire, shelling peas or listening to the crackling twigs in the stove. Our mother would smile at us, and our old nurse, Iliana, would tell us stories—some sweet and others full of ghosts and magic. We would huddle together, half-laughing, half-frightened, until the sound of a spinning wheel reminded us we were safe.

Even so, I often had trouble sleeping after such nights. Strange dreams would visit me, and I would wake up startled, too afraid to move, hiding under my blanket until the first light of dawn. But when morning came, it was as if all that fear had melted away. The fields would sparkle with frost, and thin ice would cover the pond, reflecting the rising sun's golden light. The world would feel fresh and new again.

Looking back on those times fills me with such deep emotion that I could weep like a child. The past feels so vivid and alive, but the present seems so dark and uncertain. What will happen to me? I cannot shake the feeling that this autumn will be my last. My health is failing, and I feel weaker every day.

Thedora has gone out, leaving me alone. Lately, I dread being by myself. When I sit in silence, I sometimes imagine that someone else is in the room with me, whispering things I cannot understand. It's a strange, frightening feeling, and writing to you is the only thing that seems to chase it away.

Goodbye for now. I have no more strength to write. Of the money I saved for a new dress and hat, only a single rouble remains. Yet, I am glad to hear that you were able to pay two roubles to your landlady— at least it will keep her quiet for a while. You must also repair your clothes.

Goodbye again, my dear friend. I am so tired, and I cannot understand why even the smallest task seems to drain me completely. How will I ever work again? This thought troubles me more than anything else.

Yours,

B.D.

September 5th.

My dear Barbara,

Today has been full of different experiences for me. To start, I've had a terrible headache, so by evening, I decided to take a walk along the Fontanka Canal to get some fresh air. The weather was gloomy and damp, and by six o'clock, it was already getting dark. Though it wasn't raining, there was a mist that felt like rain, and the sky was covered with heavy, trailing clouds. The street was crowded with people, all of them looking strange and miserable. There were drunken peasants stumbling along, old women with flat noses shuffling in worn slippers, bareheaded workers, cab drivers, beggars of every kind, young boys, and even a locksmith's apprentice wearing a striped smock. His thin, pale face looked like it had been scrubbed with rancid oil. I also noticed an ex-soldier trying to sell penknives and copper rings. It seemed like the kind of evening where you'd expect to meet only such people.

The canal itself was packed with boats—so many that it was hard to imagine how they all fit. On every bridge, old women were selling damp gingerbread or shriveled apples, and they all looked just as wet and dirty as the goods they were selling. Walking along the Fontanka was far from cheerful. The granite pavement was wet underfoot, the tall buildings on either side were dingy, and everything around was shrouded in mist—above, below, everywhere. The whole scene was dark and dismal tonight.

By the time I got back to Gorokhovaia Street, the sky was fully dark, and the streetlights were lit. I didn't stay there long, though, because Gorokhovaia Street is such a noisy place. But it's also incredibly luxurious. The shops and stores are magnificent, with sparkling displays of bright colors, fabrics, and hats in all sorts of shapes. It's hard to believe that these things aren't just for show. But no, people actually buy them and give them to their wives! The street is full of life, with German shopkeepers and respectable merchants selling their goods.

And the carriages! There are so many of them that it's amazing the street doesn't collapse under the weight. The carriages are splendid, with crystal-clear windows, silk and velvet interiors, and servants in fancy uniforms, some even carrying swords. I peeked into a few of them and saw women of all ages sitting inside. Maybe they were princesses or countesses. At that hour, it's likely they were on their way to balls or other grand events. It was fascinating to get such a close look at people like that—ladies so elegant and refined. I'd never seen anything quite like it before.

Then I thought of you. Oh, my dearest, my love, I often think of you, and it makes my heart ache. How is it that you are so unlucky, Barbara? Why is your life so much harder than other people's? To me, you are kind, beautiful, and smart—so why has fate been so cruel to you? How is it that someone as good as you has been left so alone, while happiness seems to come to others so easily, without any effort at all? Yes, I know—I shouldn't think this way because it's not right. But why does that cruel bird, Fate, seem to curse one person's life from the moment they are born while blessing another without reason? Sometimes it even showers blessings on someone foolish like Ivanushka. "You, foolish Ivanushka," Fate says, "will inherit your grandfather's fortune and enjoy a carefree life. But you, someone else, will only get the scraps, because that's all you deserve." I know it's wrong to think this way, but it's hard not to when these thoughts creep into my heart.

Still, it's you, my love, who should be riding in those grand carriages. Generals should be vying for your attention, and instead of wearing a simple cotton dress, you should be dressed in rich silk and glittering gold. You wouldn't look so tired and thin—you would be fresh, healthy, and as radiant as a sugar-doll. And I would be happy too—happy just to stand outside your house at night, to see the warm light from your windows and your shadow passing by. Just knowing that you were happy and well would make me the happiest man alive, my sweet little bird. But how are things really? Instead of the life you deserve, cruel people have wronged you. And then, to make things worse, some old scoundrel dares to insult you! Just because he wears a fancy coat and peers through a gold-rimmed lorgnette, he thinks he can have anything he wants—that you must put up with his condescending behavior! What an outrage!

But why is it like this? It's because you are an orphan, unprotected, without someone powerful to stand by you and give you the security you deserve. To men like him, it doesn't matter that what they're doing is vile and wrong. They don't see you as a person; they see you as an easy target. Men like that aren't men at all—they're vermin, no matter how important they think they are. I swear that even an organ-grinder I saw on Gorokhovaia Street deserves more respect than they do. At least that man works all day, even when he's hungry, and tries to earn an honest living. He wouldn't stoop to begging because he has his pride. And in his own way, he brings something good into the world. "As much as I can," he seems to say, "I'll give you a little joy." Sure, he's poor—nothing but a pauper—but at least he's an honorable one. He's tired and hungry, but he keeps going, doing what he can in his own simple way, and he earns his bread with dignity.

There are plenty of decent men like him—men whose hard work may not earn them much, but they never bow down to anyone, and they never beg. I see myself in that organ-grinder. I'm not exactly like him, of course, but in one way, I am: I do my best with what I have, and I work as hard as I can. No one can ask for more than that, and no one should expect it.

As for the organ-grinder, my dearest, I must tell you that today I had a double misfortune. While watching him play, my thoughts wandered, and I became lost in a daydream. Nearby, some cab drivers had stopped to listen as well as a young girl holding the hand of a smaller girl dressed in rags. They were all gathered to hear the music the grinder was playing beneath someone's window. Then, I noticed a little boy, about ten years old. He could have been handsome, but his face looked thin and pale. He was almost barefoot, wearing only a thin shirt, and stood there staring at the grinder, his eyes wide with wonder. He looked so pitiful.

A few other children were dancing near the music, but this boy seemed frozen. His hands and feet looked stiff from the cold, and he kept biting the end of his sleeve and shivering. I noticed he was holding a piece of paper. Soon, a man passed by and tossed a coin into the grinder's collection box, which was decorated with pictures of a Frenchman and some ladies. As the coin rattled into the box, the boy jumped, glanced around nervously, and seemed to think I was the one who had thrown it. He ran up to me, trembling, and held out the paper with shaking hands. In a broken voice, he said, "P-please sign this."

I looked at the paper and saw the usual words written on it: "Kind friends, I am a sick mother with three starving children. Please help us. Though I will soon die, if you remember my little ones in this world, I will remember you in the next." It was clear this was a desperate situation, a matter of life and death. But what could I give him? In the end, I gave him nothing, though my heart ached for him. I am certain he wasn't lying, even though he was shivering and probably starving. No, he wasn't lying.

What's truly shameful is that so many mothers fail to care for their children and send them out half-dressed into the cold. Perhaps his mother was one of those careless women who lacked any sense of responsibility. Or maybe she had no one to help her and was too sick to work. Or perhaps she was simply cruel, using her son to deceive people and beg for money.

What kind of life can a boy like that expect? Begging with a letter like that will only harden his heart. Day after day, people will ignore him or brush him off with harsh words. "Go away!" they'll say. "You're just trying to trick us." He'll hear that over and over, and his heart will grow colder. He'll shiver in the freezing air like a tiny bird that's fallen from its nest. His hands and feet will ache with cold, his breath will come in gasps, and soon enough, he'll start coughing. Sickness will creep into his fragile body like a parasite, and eventually, he'll die— probably in some dark, filthy corner where no one can help him. That's what his life will be. There are so many like him.

Oh, Barbara, it's so hard to hear someone beg "For Christ's sake!" and pass them by without giving anything. Even saying "May the Lord help you" can feel hollow. Of course, not all pleas are the same. Some are long-winded and insincere, rehearsed by those who've been begging for years. It's easier to refuse those because they feel false. You think, "This person is just playing a part. They know exactly what they're doing." But other cries for help have a raw, desperate sound that's impossible to ignore. That's how it was with the boy today.

He stood silently by the curb, saying nothing to anyone, until finally, he approached me. His voice was hoarse and broken as he whispered, "For the love of Christ, give me a penny." It startled me, and something stirred in my heart, even though I didn't give him anything. I didn't have a penny on me.

Rich people don't like hearing the cries of the poor. "They annoy us," they say. "Why should their misery disturb our peace? Why must their hunger interrupt our sleep?"

To be honest, my love, I wrote all this not just to unburden myself but also to show you the quality of my writing. You'll see that my style was developed long ago, though lately, my melancholy has crept into it. My words reflect how I feel, even though I know this won't do me much good.

Sometimes, life makes us feel worthless, as if we're no better than a rag. That's how I felt today when the boy approached me. Let me tell you a little story, my darling, and listen carefully.

Every morning, as I walk to the office, I look around at the city. I watch it waking up, lighting its fires, and preparing for the day. And when I see all this life around me, I begin to feel so small, as if someone has scolded me for my curiosity. At those moments, I shrink inside myself, my heart heavy with shame.

The truth is, if we could see inside the dark, grimy buildings of the city—if we could truly understand the lives of the people there—we would realize just how much reason there is for humility and self-reflection. Of course, I'm speaking in a figurative sense.

Let's consider what happens inside those houses. In some damp, grimy corner, perhaps in a tiny, dreary room, an artisan wakes up. All night, his dreams—if someone as unremarkable as him can dream—have been filled with thoughts of the shoes he mechanically cut out the evening before. He's a shoemaker, so his mind is consumed by his trade. Nearby, his children are crying, and his wife is hungry. He isn't the only one starting his day like this. It would hardly be worth mentioning if not for another situation. In the very same building, a wealthy person might also have spent the night dreaming of shoes, but of a much finer sort. In a way, we're all shoemakers, if you get my meaning. This, too, would be unimportant if it weren't for one thing— the wealthy person has no one to tell them, "Why do you only think of yourself? Why live only for yourself when you're not a shoemaker? Your children aren't sick. Your wife isn't hungry. Look around and find something more meaningful to occupy your thoughts than just your own comfort."

That's the point I want to make, Barbara, even though I admit it might sound a bit like free-thinking. But these ideas keep coming to me, and I can't help expressing them. So why shouldn't I sometimes feel like I'm worth no more than a penny as I listen to the constant roar and chaos of the city? Maybe you think I'm exaggerating or quoting from a book, but I'm not. I hate exaggeration, I have no use for whims, and I'm not borrowing anyone else's words.

Today I came home feeling sad. I sat down at the table, made myself some tea, and was about to drink a second glass when Gorshkov, the poor lodger, came into my room. Earlier that morning, I'd noticed him wandering around the other lodgers, as though trying to speak to someone, including me. His situation is far worse than mine. Just think—he has a wife and children! If I were in his shoes, I don't know how I would manage. He entered, bowed awkwardly, and stood there with pus on his eyelashes as usual, his feet shuffling nervously, and his tongue struggling to form words. I motioned for him to sit in a chair—it was old and falling apart, but it was the only one I had—and offered him some tea. At first, he refused. He kept refusing, but eventually, he gave in. Then he wanted to drink the tea without sugar and apologized repeatedly, but I insisted he take some. After much hesitation, he finally accepted the smallest lump and insisted it was sweet enough. How deeply poverty humbles a person!

"Well, what is it?" I asked him gently. "What can I do for you?" He looked at me and said, "Makar Alexievitch, you've helped me before. Please, I beg you, show me mercy again and help my family. My wife and children have nothing to eat. Imagine a father being forced to say that!" I was about to reply, but he cut me off. "I'm afraid to ask the other lodgers," he explained. "It's not that I fear them exactly, but I'm ashamed. They're proud and stuck-up. I wouldn't have come to you either, my kind friend and benefactor, except that I know you've had

119

your own troubles and debts. That's why I dared to ask you—you're kind-hearted and can understand my suffering."

He apologized for troubling me and for being so awkward. I told him I would love to help, but I had nothing to give. "Ah, Makar Alexievitch," he said, "surely I'm not asking for much. My wife and children are starving. Could you spare just ten kopecks?" My heart clenched at his words. "How these people shame me," I thought. But I only had twenty kopecks left, and I'd been saving them for my own needs. "I can't, my friend," I said, shaking my head. "Well, whatever you can spare," he pleaded. "Even just five kopecks?" In the end, I opened my cash box and gave him all twenty. It was the right thing to do. But to think such poverty exists!

We talked a bit more. I asked him why he had rented a room for five roubles when he was in such dire straits. He explained that when he first moved in six months ago, he paid three months' rent upfront. Since then, his situation had worsened and never improved. He told me how he had been sued by a merchant who had defrauded the government in a contract. Though Gorshkov had only been careless and hadn't stolen anything, the fraud dragged him into the mess. Years passed, and his reputation was ruined. He was dismissed from his job and couldn't recover the large sum of money the merchant owed him, even though the courts had partially ruled in his favor.

I believe Gorshkov's story. The situation is so tangled that even a hundred years wouldn't be enough to unravel it. Though parts of it have been resolved, the merchant still holds all the power. Meanwhile, Gorshkov struggles to survive. He has no job and no resources, yet he refuses to give up hope. Another child has recently been born, adding to the family's expenses, and one of his other children recently died, which brought even more costs. His wife is in poor health, and he himself has been sick for years. He has suffered so much, yet he remains confident that things will eventually work out.

I felt terrible for him and tried to comfort him as best I could. He came to me for solace, and I wanted to ease his burden, even if only a little.

Goodbye, my dear Barbara. May Christ protect you and keep you healthy. Thinking of you is like a balm for my soul. Though I suffer for you, I do so willingly and with love.

Your true friend,

Makar Dievushkin.

September 9th.

My dearest Barbara Alexievna,

I am overwhelmed as I write to you, for something terrible has happened. My mind is spinning. Oh, my beloved, how can I explain it to you? I never imagined this could occur. But no—that's not entirely true. Perhaps I did sense it coming, because I once had a dream that felt strangely similar to this.

Let me tell you everything, simply and truthfully, as it happened. Today, I went to the office as usual and sat down to work. You should know that I had been working on something similar the day before, and during that time, Timothei Ivanovitch came to me with an urgent request. "Makar Alexievitch," he said, "please copy this document for me quickly and carefully. It needs to be signed today."

Now, yesterday I wasn't feeling well at all. I was troubled, weighed down by a heavy sadness. My chest felt tight, and my thoughts were clouded. I couldn't focus on anything because my mind kept drifting to you, my dear. Even so, I set to work on the document and copied it neatly. But somehow—whether the devil confused me, fate willed it, or it was simply inevitable—I left out an entire line! This mistake turned the whole thing into nonsense.

The document had been given to me too late to be signed last night, so it was submitted to his Excellency this morning. When I arrived at the office, I took my usual seat beside Emelia Ivanovitch. Lately, I've been feeling more nervous and self-conscious than ever before. It's hard for me to look anyone in the eye. Even the sound of a chair creaking can make my heart race. Today, I slumped into my seat, trying to make myself as small as possible.

Efim Akimovitch, who is quick to take offense over the smallest things, leaned over and whispered, "Why are you sitting like that, Makar Alexievitch?" Then he pulled such a ridiculous face that everyone around us burst out laughing. They laughed at me. I tried to block it out, covering my ears, frowning, and sitting completely still. That's the only way I know to make their laughter stop.

Suddenly, I heard a commotion—a bustle of movement and the sound of someone running. Then I realized I was being called, loudly and urgently. My heart began to pound in my chest. I didn't know why, but I was terrified, more so than I've ever been in my life. I clung to my chair, feeling paralyzed, as the voices drew closer. They were shouting my name: "Dievushkin! Dievushkin! Where is Dievushkin?"

Finally, I looked up and saw Evstafi Ivanovitch standing before me. "Makar Alexievitch," he said, "you must go to his Excellency immediately. There's been a mistake in a document." That was all he said, but it was enough to fill me with dread. I felt cold as ice, like my body had gone numb. Somehow, I managed to rise from my seat and make my way to where I had been summoned.

I walked through one room, then another, then a third, until I reached his Excellency's office. I can't clearly recall what I was thinking during those moments. My mind was blank. All I remember is seeing his Excellency standing there, surrounded by several people. I'm not sure if I even greeted him—I probably forgot to. I was so panicked that my teeth were chattering, and my knees were trembling.

First, I felt deeply ashamed of how I looked. There was a mirror on the wall to my right, and when I caught a glimpse of my reflection, I was horrified. Second, I felt completely insignificant. I've always tried to behave as though I don't exist, to go unnoticed. I doubt his Excellency even knew I worked in his department. Perhaps he had heard my name in passing, but he certainly had never interacted with me before.

He began angrily: "What have you done here? Why aren't you more careful? This document was needed quickly, and you've ruined it. What do you think of this?" That last question was directed at Evstafi Ivanovitch. I didn't hear much else, just bits and pieces like "Such carelessness!" and "How clumsy this is!" and so on. I tried to say something, to beg for forgiveness, but the words wouldn't come. I didn't even dare to leave the room.

Then something happened that fills me with shame even now as I write. A button of mine—the devil take it!—that had been hanging by a thread, suddenly popped off. It hopped and rolled noisily across the floor, stopping right at the feet of his Excellency. All this happened in complete silence! This ridiculous button was my only answer to my superior!

What happened next makes me shudder to recall. His Excellency's attention turned toward me, and for the first time, he truly looked at me—at my shabby figure and ragged clothes. I remembered what I had seen in the mirror earlier and felt utterly humiliated. Determined to retrieve the button, I scrambled after it. It kept rolling and slipping away, and the more I fumbled, the more foolish I looked. I was completely helpless. I felt my strength leaving me, and with it, my last shred of dignity. It was as if I could hear the voices of Theresa and Phaldoni mocking me in my ears.

At last, I managed to grab the button. Straightening myself, I stood with my hands clasped, feeling like a complete fool. I tried to reattach the button, fumbling with the loose threads and smiling nervously every time it fell off again. At first, his Excellency turned away, but then he glanced at me again and said to Evstafi Ivanovitch, "What's wrong with him? Look at the state he's in! Who is this man?"

Oh, Barbara, just to hear those words—"Who is this man?"—was enough to make me feel like a marked man, someone singled out for scorn. Evstafi murmured in reply, "He's of no particular importance, though he has a good character. His salary is modest but sufficient."

"Very well," said his Excellency. "Help him sort this out. Give him an advance on his salary."

"It's already been advanced," replied Evstafi. "He received it some time ago. But his record is clean; there's nothing against him."

At that moment, I felt as if I were standing in the flames of hell. I wanted to vanish, to disappear completely. "Well, well," said his Excellency. "Let him redo the document. Dievushkin, come here. Copy this again, and do it quickly." Then he turned away to give orders to the other officials in the room, and the group dispersed.

Once everyone had left, his Excellency pulled out his pocketbook, took out a hundred-rouble note, and handed it to me, saying, "Take this. It's all I can give. Use it as you need."

I was so moved, Barbara, I could barely stand. My hands trembled as I reached for the note. Without thinking, I grabbed his Excellency's hand in gratitude. To my astonishment, he blushed but didn't pull away. No, I swear to you, Barbara, he didn't. Instead, he shook my hand as though I were his equal, as though I were a general like himself! "Go now," he said kindly. "That's all I can do for you. Just make sure you don't make any more mistakes."

Barbara, I ask you and Thedora—and if I had children, I would ask them too—to pray for his Excellency every day. I would say to them, "You don't need to pray for me, but pray for him until the end of your lives."

Even during these painful days when I've been crushed by the sight of your poverty and my own failures, I don't value the hundred roubles as much as I value his kindness. By shaking my hand, he restored my dignity and gave me back my will to live. That single act filled my life with sweetness and hope. I am certain that, though I am a sinner, my prayers for his Excellency's happiness will reach the throne of heaven.

But, my dearest, at this moment I feel overwhelmed and shaken. My heart is pounding as though it will burst, and I feel weak all over. I am sending you forty-five roubles. I will give twenty to my landlady and keep thirty-five for myself—twenty for new clothes and fifteen for daily expenses.

The events of this morning have left me completely exhausted. It's quiet here now, very quiet, but I can feel my breath trembling deep in my chest. I'll come to see you soon, my treasure, but for now, my head aches with everything I've been through. God sees all, my darling, my priceless one.

Your steadfast friend,

Makar Dievushkin.

September 10th.

My beloved Makar Alexievitch,

I am overjoyed by your good fortune and deeply appreciate the kindness of your superior. Now, take some time to rest and free yourself from worries. But please, don't spend money needlessly again. Live as quietly and frugally as possible, and from this day forward, make it a habit to save something for the future so that misfortune doesn't catch you off guard again.

Please, for God's sake, don't worry about us—Thedora and I will manage somehow. Why did you send me so much money? I truly don't need it; what I already had would have been more than enough. It's true that I will soon need more money to move out of these lodgings, but Thedora is expecting to receive repayment of an old debt soon. Of course, at least twenty roubles will have to be set aside for basic necessities, but the rest will be returned to you. Please take good care of it, Makar Alexievitch.

Now, goodbye. I hope your life remains peaceful and that you stay healthy and in good spirits. I would have written more, but I'm feeling terribly exhausted. I didn't even get out of bed yesterday. I'm glad you promised to come visit me. Yes, you absolutely must come.

B. D.

September 11th.

My darling Barbara Alexievna,

I beg you, please don't leave me now that I'm happy and content again. Ignore whatever Thedora says, and I'll do anything in the world for you. I'll behave better, if only out of respect for his Excellency, and I'll carefully watch everything I do. We'll go back to exchanging cheerful letters, sharing our thoughts, joys, and even sorrows—though I hope we won't have any more sorrows. We'll live twice as happily and comfortably as we used to. We can even exchange books again.

My angel, a great change has come to my life—a very good one. My landlady has become more pleasant, Theresa has regained her senses, and even Phaldoni is eager to do as I ask. I've also made peace with Rataziaev. He came to visit me as soon as he heard the good news. It turns out he's a good man, and all those rumors about him were untrue. For one thing, I discovered he never had any intention of putting us into his book—he told me that himself. He even read me his latest work. As for calling me "Lovelace," he meant no offense. It's just a word borrowed from another language that means something like a clever man or, in more refined terms, a gentleman of importance. It was only a harmless joke, my dear. I misunderstood and got upset for no reason, so I apologized to him.

The weather today is beautiful, Barbara! There was a little frost in the morning, like it had been sifted through a sieve, but it didn't last long. A breeze soon freshened the air. I went out to buy a pair of shoes and got a wonderful pair. Afterward, I took a walk along the Nevski Prospect and read The Daily Bee. That reminds me—I almost forgot to tell you the most important thing.

This morning, I had a conversation with Emelia Ivanovitch and Aksenti Michaelovitch about his Excellency. Apparently, I'm not the only person he has helped. Everyone knows him for his kindness. People praise him everywhere, and many have shed tears of gratitude because of him. For instance, he once took care of an orphaned girl, married her to an official who was the son of a poor widow, and found a job for the man in a government office. He even helped them in other ways. Hearing this, I felt it was my duty to tell my own story of his Excellency's kindness. So, I shared the whole tale with my companions, leaving out no details.

Why should I be ashamed of feeling proud about it? "Let everyone hear about this," I thought. "It will bring honor to his Excellency." I spoke with enthusiasm and didn't hold back. I even told everyone present, including my landlady, Phaldoni, Rataziaev, and Markov, about my new shoes! Some people laughed at me—probably because of how I looked or because of the shoe story—but I'm sure they didn't mean any harm. They were probably just young or well-off, and their laughter wasn't malicious. Don't you think so, Barbara?

Even now, I'm struggling to pull myself together after all that's happened. Do you have enough firewood, Barbara? Please don't let yourself get cold. Your worries about the future have weighed on my heart. Every day, I pray to God for you—how fervently I pray! Also, do you have warm clothes, like woolen stockings? If there's anything you need, please don't hurt this old man's feelings by not asking me. The hard times are over now, and the future looks bright.

But those hard times, Barbara—they were terrible, even though they're behind us now. As time goes on, we'll rebuild our lives. I can still vividly recall my youth. I never had a single kopeck to spare, yet I was always cheerful. I'd walk along the Nevski Prospect, seeing well-dressed people, and feel happy all day. Life was so wonderful back then, especially in St. Petersburg! Just yesterday, I was on my knees, begging

God to forgive my sins during those dark days—for my complaints, my despair, my gambling, and my drunkenness. And I prayed for you, too, because you've always supported me. You've given me advice and encouragement, and I'll never forget that.

Today, I kissed each one of your letters. Goodbye for now, my dearest. I've heard there's a clothing sale nearby, so I'll check it out. Once again, goodbye, my angel.

Yours in heart and soul,

Makar Dievushkin.

September 15th.

My dearest Makar Alexievitch,

I am in terrible distress and feel certain that something bad is about to happen. The issue, my dear friend, is that Monsieur Bwikov is back in St. Petersburg. Thedora has seen him. She said he was riding in a drozhki, but when he saw her, he told the driver to stop, jumped out, and asked her where she was living. Thedora refused to tell him, but he smiled and said he already knew who was staying with her—it seems Anna Thedorovna must have told him. At that, Thedora couldn't hold back any longer and scolded him right there on the street, calling him immoral and blaming him for all my misfortunes.

He responded by saying that someone without a penny to her name must surely be in a bad state. Thedora replied that I could always earn a living with my own hands or even marry, and that it wasn't just about losing jobs, but about losing my happiness, which had nearly destroyed me. Then he said something cruel, claiming that while I was still young, I seemed to have lost my senses, and that my "virtue appeared to be under a cloud"—those were his exact words.

Both Thedora and I had thought he didn't know where I lived, but last night, just as I had gone out to do some shopping at Gostinni Dvor, he came to our rooms. It seemed like he had deliberately chosen a time when I wouldn't be home. He asked Thedora many questions about how we were living. After looking over my work, he asked, "Who is this civil servant friend of yours?" At that moment, you happened to walk through the courtyard, so Thedora pointed you out. He stared at you and laughed. Thedora told him to leave, saying that I was still unwell from grief and that seeing him would upset me greatly. After pausing, he replied that he had only come because he had nothing

131

better to do. He even tried to give Thedora twenty-five roubles, but of course, she refused.

What does this mean? Why did he come? I can't figure out how he found out about me, and it's driving me mad. Thedora thinks it might have something to do with her sister-in-law Aksinia, who visits sometimes. Aksinia knows a laundress named Nastasia, and Nastasia has a cousin who works as a watchman in the same department where a friend of Anna Thedorovna's nephew works. Could this be the connection? Could something have been planned through these people? But Thedora might be wrong—we really don't know what to think.

What if he comes again? The thought terrifies me. When Thedora told me about his visit last night, I was so frightened that I almost fainted. What could this man want? I don't want anything to do with people like him. What could they possibly want from someone as wretched as me? I can't stop worrying, constantly feeling like Bwikov is just around the corner. What will happen to me? What more does fate have in store for me?

For Christ's sake, come and see me, Makar Alexievitch! Please, come soon—I need you!

B. D.

September 18th.

My beloved Barbara Alexievna,

Today, something tragic, unexpected, and mysterious happened in this house. First, let me tell you that poor Gorshkov has finally been cleared of all guilt. The decision took a long time, but this morning he went to hear the final ruling, and it was completely in his favor. Any accusations against him for negligence or wrongdoing were dismissed, and he was also granted the right to recover a large sum of money from the merchant. His name has been cleared, his honor restored, and he could not have asked for a more favorable outcome.

When he came home at three o'clock, he looked pale as a ghost, and his lips were trembling, but he was smiling as he embraced his wife and children. We all rushed to congratulate him, and he was deeply moved by our kindness. He bowed to each of us and shook our hands one by one. I noticed that he seemed taller and stood straighter than before, and the usual drops of pus were gone from his eyelashes. Yet, he was clearly very agitated. He couldn't sit still for even two minutes, constantly picking things up and putting them down, bowing, smiling, sitting, standing, and talking endlessly about his honor, his good name, and his family. He talked so much—and he cried, too. It was hard for any of us to hold back our own tears.

Rataziaev, trying to encourage him, remarked that honor didn't matter much when someone had nothing to eat, and that money was the most important thing in the world. He even said that only money was worth thanking God for. Then he slapped Gorshkov on the shoulder. I thought Gorshkov seemed hurt by this. He didn't say anything directly, but he gave Rataziaev a strange look and gently brushed his hand off his shoulder. In the past, he wouldn't have done that, but people react differently in moments like this. For example, I myself might have hesitated to show any pride during such a joyful time, even though being overly humble could also be seen as weak. But that's none of my business. All Gorshkov said was, "Yes, money is a good thing. Glory be to God!" He kept repeating, "Glory be to God, glory be to God!" the whole time we were in his room.

His wife decided to prepare a nicer meal than usual, and even the landlady helped cook it. Despite her flaws, she isn't a bad woman at heart. But until the meal was ready, Gorshkov couldn't stay still. He went into everyone's room, whether he was invited or not, sat down with a smile, sometimes said something, and sometimes just got up and left without a word. In the naval officer's room, he picked up a deck of cards and was invited to join a game, but after losing a few times and making some mistakes, he gave up. "No," he said, "that's the kind of man I am—that's all I'm good for," and left.

Later, I met him in the hallway. He took my hands, looked at me with an odd expression, pressed my hands again, and walked away still smiling—but it was a strange, tired smile, almost like the smile of a dead man. Meanwhile, his wife was crying with joy, and their room was decorated like it was a holiday. When dinner was finally served, Gorshkov ate with his family, and afterward, he told his wife, "Now, my dear, I'm going to rest for a while." Then he went to bed.

As he lay down, he called his little daughter to his side, placed his hand on her head, and looked at her for a long time. Then he asked his wife, "What about Petinka? Where is our Petinka?" His wife crossed herself and said, "Why, our Petinka is dead." "Yes, yes, I know," Gorshkov replied. "Petinka is now in the Kingdom of Heaven." This made his wife realize that he wasn't entirely himself—that the day's events had overwhelmed him. "My love, you should sleep for a while," she said. "I will," he answered. "Right away—I'm feeling a little—" And then he turned over and fell silent. A little later, he tried to say

134

something else, but his wife couldn't hear him. "What are you saying?" she asked, but he didn't reply.

Thinking he had fallen asleep, she left the room to spend an hour with the landlady. When she returned, he was still lying motionless. "He's sleeping so soundly," she thought as she sat down to do some work. She told us later that she lost track of time and fell into a sort of daydream. She couldn't remember what she had been thinking, but she realized she had completely forgotten about her husband. Then, suddenly, a strange feeling came over her. The room was eerily quiet. She looked at the bed and saw that he was still lying in the same position. She pulled back the covers and found him cold and stiff. He had died suddenly, as if struck down in an instant. What exactly caused his death, only God knows.

This event has shaken me so much that I can't gather my thoughts. It's hard to believe that someone can die so simply—and he was such a poor, unfortunate man, this Gorshkov! What a fate! His wife is devastated, crying endlessly, and their little daughter has run off to hide somewhere. Their room is in chaos, as the doctors are preparing to perform an autopsy. I can't tell you everything for sure; I only know that I feel incredibly sad. It's heartbreaking to think how little control we have over what might happen in a single day—or even a single hour.

Your own,

Makar Dievushkin.

September 19th.

My beloved Barbara Alexievna,

I'm writing to let you know that Rataziaev has found some work for me. He introduced me to a writer who has given him a large manuscript, and now I've been tasked with copying it. Glory be to God—this means I'll have a lot of work to do! However, even though the job is urgent, the manuscript is so poorly written that I hardly know how to begin. Some parts of it are almost impossible to read.

I've agreed to do the work for forty kopecks per sheet. So, as you can see—and this is the real reason I wanted to write to you—we will soon have money coming in from an additional source.

Goodbye for now; I need to get started on my work.

Your sincere friend,

Makar Dievushkin.

September 23rd.

My dearest Makar Alexievitch,

I haven't written to you for the past three days because I've been so worried and upset. Three days ago, Bwikov came to see me again. I was alone at the time since Thedora had gone out. When I opened the door and saw him, I was so frightened that I froze in place and felt myself go pale. He came in laughing loudly, took a chair, and sat down. I couldn't collect my thoughts; I just sat there silently, trying to continue my work.

After a while, his smile faded. I think my appearance surprised him. Over the past year, I've become so thin, my cheeks hollow, my eyes sunken, and my face pale as a sheet. I doubt anyone who knew me before would recognize me now. After staring at me for a long time, he seemed to recover his spirits. He said something, and I replied as best I could. Then he laughed again. He stayed for a whole hour, talking to me and asking questions about different things.

Just before leaving, he took my hand and said—these were his exact words—"Between us, Barbara Alexievna, that relative of yours, Anna Thedorovna, is a truly wicked woman." He even used a more vulgar term to describe her. "First, she led your cousin astray, and then she ruined you. I admit I've behaved like a scoundrel too, but that's how the world is." He laughed again. Then he said that, although he wasn't very eloquent, he felt it was his duty as a gentleman to have a clear and honest conversation with me.

He told me he wanted to marry me. He said it was his responsibility to restore my honor. He promised me wealth and said that after we married, he would take me to his estate in the countryside, where we could go hare hunting. He added that he would never return to St.

Petersburg because he despised the city and had a worthless nephew he intended to disinherit in favor of a proper heir. Finally, he said that finding a legal heir was the main reason he wanted to marry me.

He remarked that I seemed to be living in poor conditions—though he said this was not surprising, given the "kennel" I lived in. He told me I would not survive another month in such a place, and that all lodgings in St. Petersburg were horrible. Then he asked if I needed anything.

I was so shocked by his proposal that I could only burst into tears. He took this as a sign of gratitude and told me he had always admired my sense, intelligence, and sensitivity. However, he explained, he hadn't approached me earlier because he wanted to see how I was managing. He asked some questions about you, saying he'd heard you were an honorable man and wanted to settle his "debt" to you. He offered five hundred roubles, asking if that would be enough to repay you for everything you'd done for me. I told him your kindness could never be repaid with money. He dismissed this, calling it nonsense, and said I must still be young enough to read too much poetry. He argued that romantic ideas like that were what ruined young women, and that books only corrupted morals. "Live as long as I have," he said, "and then you'll see what people are really like."

He asked me to think carefully about his proposal, saying he didn't want me to make a hasty decision. He warned that impulsive choices could ruin someone as inexperienced as me, but he hoped I would accept. "If not," he added, "I'll have to marry a merchant's daughter in Moscow to ensure my nephew doesn't inherit." Then he pressed five hundred roubles into my hand, saying it was for "bonbons," and told me that in the countryside, I'd grow plump and happy. He explained he was very busy but had taken the time to visit me, and then he left.

For a long time after he left, I sat in deep thought. Even though my mind was troubled, I eventually made a decision. My dear friend, I'm going to marry this man. I have no other choice. If anyone can save me from this misery, restore my honor, and protect me from future poverty and suffering, it's him. What else can I expect from life? What else can I hope for? Thedora says one should never give up on happiness, but I ask her—what happiness can there be for someone like me?

I can't keep working like this. My health is ruined. I'm a shadow of myself and no longer capable of much. If I try to go on, I'll only become a burden to others. No, this marriage won't bring me paradise, but what other option do I have? What other path is open to me?

I didn't ask for your advice earlier because I needed to think this through on my own. But my decision is final. I'm about to give my answer to Bwikov, who has been pressing me for a reply. He says his business can't wait, and he needs to leave soon. Only God knows whether this choice will bring me happiness, but my fate is in His hands. Bwikov is said to be kind-hearted. At the very least, he'll respect me, and maybe I'll learn to respect him. What more could I ask for in a marriage like this?

I've told you everything, Makar Alexievitch, and I trust you'll understand my despair. Please don't try to change my mind—it won't do any good. Think carefully about everything that has led me to this decision. My anguish was terrible at first, but now I feel calmer. Whatever happens is in God's hands.

Bwikov has just arrived, so I must finish this letter. There was much more I wanted to say, but he's at the door now.

Yours,

Barbara Alexievna.

September 23rd.

My beloved Barbara Alexievna,

I'm writing to reply to your letter right away—I can't tell you how astonished I am. By the way, I should mention that yesterday we buried poor Gorshkov. Yes, Bwikov has acted nobly, and it seems you have no choice but to accept him. Everything is in God's hands. That is how it has always been and always will be. The ways of our Creator are both good and beyond our understanding, just as Fate, which is one with Him, is mysterious.

Thedora will share in your happiness because, of course, you will be happy. You'll be free from want, my darling, dearest, sweetest angel! But why must this be so rushed? Oh, yes—I suppose it's because of Monsieur Bwikov's business affairs. Only a man with no responsibilities could afford to ignore such things.

I caught a glimpse of Monsieur Bwikov as he was leaving your door. He's a very fine-looking man—very fine indeed. But I admit that wasn't the first thing I noticed, as I wasn't quite myself at the time.

Will we still be able to write to each other in the future? I keep wondering what has led you to say all that you did in your letter. And to think, just as I had finished copying twenty pages, this news arrives!

I suppose now you'll be able to buy many things—shoes, dresses, and all sorts of items. Do you remember the shops on Gorokhovaia Street that I used to tell you about? But no, you shouldn't go out right now. You absolutely mustn't. Soon enough, you'll be able to buy all the things you want and even keep a carriage. But for now, the weather is terrible. The rain is pouring down like buckets, soaking everything. You might catch a cold in this weather, my darling, and it could harm your health. Why risk it when I'm here to help you?

So, Thedora thinks great happiness awaits you? She's such a chatterbox and always meddling in things. Does she want to ruin you?

Will you be going to the all-night Mass this evening, my dearest? I'd like to come and see you there. Bwikov was right when he said you're a woman of virtue, wit, and good character. But I still think he'd be better off marrying that merchant's daughter. What do you think about that? Yes, it would be a much better match for him.

As soon as it gets dark tonight, I'll come and sit with you for an hour. Twilight will fall early, so I'll be there soon. Whatever happens, I need to see you, even if it's just for a little while. I suppose you're expecting Bwikov now, but I'll come as soon as he leaves. Please stay home until I arrive, my dearest.

Makar Dievushkin.

September 27th.

Dear Makar Alexievitch,

Bwikov has just told me that I need at least three dozen linen blouses, so I have to find some seamstresses immediately to make two dozen of them, since time is running out. Monsieur Bwikov is quite frustrated with all the fuss over these details, especially since there are only five days left until the wedding, and we're leaving the day after. He keeps rushing around, saying there's no time to waste on such trifles.

I'm terribly stressed and can barely stand on my feet. There's so much to do, and perhaps too much that doesn't even need to be done! On top of that, I don't have any blond lace or other trimmings, so I'll need to purchase those too. Bwikov insists that his bride cannot look like a servant—his words—and that I must "outshine the great ladies." That's exactly how he put it.

I need you to go to Madame Chiffon's on Gorokhovaia Street. First, please ask her to send me some seamstresses, and second, request that she come herself, as I'm too unwell to leave the house. Our new apartment is freezing cold and still a complete mess. Also, Bwikov has an elderly aunt who is on the brink of death. She might pass away before we leave, but Bwikov insists it's nothing serious and that she'll recover soon.

He's not staying with me yet, so I have to run all over the place to find him. The only help I have is from Thedora and Bwikov's valet, who supervises everything but hasn't been around for three days. Each morning, Bwikov goes to his business, and he's constantly losing his temper. Just yesterday, he got into trouble with the police for hitting the steward of this building.

I don't have anyone to deliver this letter, so I'll send it through the post. Oh! I almost forgot the most important thing. Please tell Madame Chiffon that I want the blond lace changed to match the patterns I showed her yesterday, and that she should bring a new selection. Also, let her know I've changed my mind about the satin. I now want it embroidered with crochet work, and the embroidery should include monograms on the garments. Make sure you tell her it must be embroidered, not plain. Do you hear me? Embroidered, not plain.

One more thing—I almost forgot again! The lappets on the fur cloak need to be adjusted, and the collar should be edged with lace. Please make sure you tell her all of this, Makar Alexievitch.

Your friend,

B. D.

P.S.—I'm so embarrassed to keep troubling you with all these errands! This is the third morning you've spent running around for me. But what else can I do? The apartment is in such chaos, and I'm not feeling well. Please don't be angry with me, Makar Alexievitch. I'm feeling so low. What's going to happen to me, my dear, kind friend? I feel so uneasy, as if I'm living in a fog. Please, for God's sake, don't forget any of these instructions. I'm so worried you might make a mistake. Remember, everything must be embroidered, not plain.

September 27th.

My beloved Barbara Alexievna,

I have carefully carried out all your requests. Madame Chiffon mentioned that she had already thought of using tambour work, as she believed it to be more suitable (though I didn't quite follow everything she said). She also told me that since you provided specific instructions in writing, she has followed them exactly (though, again, I can't remember all of her words clearly—I just know she talked a lot, as she is quite a tiresome woman). She will soon repeat all of this to you in person.

As for me, I feel utterly exhausted and didn't even go to the office today. But don't lose hope about the future, my dearest. If it would save you any trouble, I'd visit every shop in St. Petersburg for you. You wrote that you're afraid to think about what lies ahead, but by tonight, at seven o'clock, everything will become clear. Madame Chiffon herself will come to see you. Hold on to hope, and everything will work out for the best. Of course, I'm only talking about these frustrating little details—these frills and decorations!

Oh, how much I want to see you, my angel! Yes, how happy I would be to see you. Twice today I've walked past the gates of your home. Unfortunately, this Bwikov is such a quick-tempered man that—well, things are what they are.

Makar Dievushkin.

September 28th.

My dearest Makar Alexievitch,

For God's sake, please go to the jeweler and tell him that he doesn't need to make the pearl and emerald earrings after all. Monsieur Bwikov says they are too expensive and will cost him far too much—he says they'll burn a hole in his pocket. He's lost his temper again and claims that he's being cheated. Yesterday, he even said that if he had known or anticipated these expenses, he would never have agreed to marry.

He also mentioned that, given the situation, he only plans to have a simple wedding and leave immediately afterward. "Don't expect any dancing, celebrations, or entertaining of guests," he said. "Our grand times are still far off." Those were his exact words. God knows I don't want such things, but even so, Bwikov has forbidden them. I didn't respond because he gets irritated so easily.

What is going to happen to me?

B. D.

September 28th.

My beloved Barbara Alexievna,

The matter with the jeweler has been taken care of. Unfortunately, I need to tell you that I've fallen ill and can't get out of bed. Just when there's so much to do, I've gone and caught a chill—curse it all!

To make things worse, his Excellency has decided to become stricter. Today, he scolded poor Emelia Ivanovitch so harshly that the man was completely shaken. That's all the news I have to share.

Actually, there's something else I'd like to write about, but I'm afraid it might bother you. I'm just a simple, foolish man who writes down whatever comes to mind.

Your friend,

Makar Dievushkin.

September 29th.

My own Barbara Alexievna,

Today, my dearest, I saw Thedora, who told me that you are getting married tomorrow and leaving the following day. Bwikov has already arranged for a post-chaise to take you away.

I've already told you about the matter with his Excellency. Also, I checked the bill from the shop on Gorokhovaia Street—it's accurate but very long. Why is Monsieur Bwikov so upset with you? But no, you must stay cheerful, my darling. I will remain cheerful too, as long as you are happy.

I wanted to come to the church tomorrow, but unfortunately, the pain in my back won't let me. I also thought of writing an account of the ceremony, but there will be no one to share the details with me.

You have been so kind to Thedora, my dearest. You've treated her with such care and generosity. For deeds like that, God will bless you. Good deeds are never forgotten, and virtue will always be rewarded, whether sooner or later. I wish I could write so much more to you. I feel like I could write to you endlessly. Every hour, every moment could be spent writing to you.

Only your book, The Stories of Bielkin, is left with me. Please don't take it away—I beg you to let me keep it. It's not just that I want to read the book itself, but with winter coming, the evenings will be long and lonely, and I'll need something to read, even if it's just a little.

Did I tell you that I'm planning to move into your old apartment? I intend to rent it from Thedora. I can't bear the thought of parting with that good woman, and besides, she's such a wonderful worker. Yesterday, I went to look at your empty room. I carefully examined everything. Your embroidery frame is still in its corner, with the unfinished work hanging on it, just as you left it. I even found one of my letters being used as a spool for thread. On the table, there was a scrap of paper with the words, "My dearest Makar Alexievitch, I hasten to—" but nothing more. Clearly, something interrupted you while you were writing.

Behind a screen, I found your little bed. Oh, my darling, my dearest one!

Goodbye for now—yes, goodbye. But please, for God's sake, send me something in reply to this letter.

Makar Dievushkin.

September 30th.

My beloved Makar Alexievitch,

It's done! My fate is sealed! I don't know what lies ahead for me, but I am submitting to God's will. Tomorrow, we leave. For the last time, I bid you farewell, my priceless friend, my benefactor, my dearest one. Please don't grieve for me. Try to live happily and think of me sometimes. May God's blessings shine upon you! I will always remember you and include you in my prayers.

Our time together has come to an end. My new life will bring me little comfort from memories of the past. Because of that, I will treasure your memory even more, and you will always remain dear to my heart. Here, you were my only friend. Here, you were the only one who truly loved me. Yes, I have seen and known everything—you have loved me deeply, and I have always felt it. A single smile from me or a few words from my pen could make you happy. But now you must forget me.

How lonely you will be! Why should you stay here, my kind and irreplaceable friend? I am leaving my book, the embroidery frame, and the unfinished letter in your care. When you see the few words written on that letter, you will know in your heart everything I wanted to say but couldn't. Think of your little Barbara sometimes, the one who loved you so much. I've left all your letters in the top drawer of Thedora's chest.

You wrote that you're unwell, but Monsieur Bwikov won't let me leave the house today, so I can only write to you. I promise to write again soon, but only God knows when I'll be able to. For now, we must say goodbye forever, my beloved, my friend, my own! Yes, forever! Oh, how I wish I could embrace you at this moment! Goodbye, dear friend—goodbye! May you always be well and happy. I will keep you in my prayers until the end. My heart is heavy with sorrow. Monsieur Bwikov is calling for me now.

Your ever-loving,

B.

P.S.—My heart is overflowing. It's breaking with tears and sorrow, tearing me apart. Goodbye. My God, what pain! Please, please don't forget your poor Barbara.

My dearest Barbara, my jewel, my priceless one,

You are about to leave! You're almost on your way! How I wish they had taken my heart instead of you. How could you let this happen? You're crying, yet you're leaving! And just now, I've received a letter from you, soaked with your tears. You must be going against your will. You must be sorry for me. You must love me!

But how will you manage now? Your heart will grow cold, sick, and heavy. Grief will drain the life out of it, tear it apart. You'll die where you are, and they'll bury you in the cold, wet earth with no one to mourn you. Meanwhile, Bwikov will be out hunting hares.

Oh, my darling! Why did you make this decision? How could you take this step? What have you done? What have you done? Soon, they'll carry you to your grave. Soon, your beauty will fade, my angel. You're so fragile, like a feather.

Where have I been all this time? What was I thinking? I treated you like a child with a simple headache, blind to what was happening. Fool that I am! I acted like it was none of my concern. I ran around worrying about meaningless things.

But I will get up. Tomorrow, I will rise, sound and strong. I will be myself again. Dearest, I would throw myself under a carriage rather than see you leave like this. How can they do this?

150

I'll go with you. I'll follow your carriage if you won't take me. I'll run until I have no breath left. Do you even know where you're going? The Steppes, my darling. Only the Steppes. A barren, empty land. The trees have already lost their leaves, and there's nothing but cold and rain.

Why are you going there? Bwikov will have his amusements, but what about you? Do you want to live as a lonely estate lady? Look at yourself, my angel. You're not made for that life. Who will I write to? Who will I call "my dearest"? Where will I find you?

When you're gone, I'll die. I can't bear this misery. I love you as I love the light of God. I've devoted all my love to you. I've lived only because you were near. Every letter I wrote, every word I copied—it was all for you. Did you know that?

Please don't leave. It's impossible, utterly impossible. The rain will soak you, and you'll fall ill. Your carriage will break down; it's inevitable. Here, in St. Petersburg, they build carriages poorly. They don't last.

I'll go to Bwikov and beg him. I'll tell him everything. Please, dearest, tell him you can't leave. Let him marry that merchant's daughter in Moscow. She's better suited for him. What is he to you? He buys trinkets, but what are they? They're meaningless compared to life.

As soon as I get my next salary, I'll buy you a new cloak. Just wait a little longer, my angel. God, why are you leaving for the Steppes with Bwikov? Why, knowing you won't come back?

But you must write to me. Promise me one last letter, even if it's truly the last. How has it come to this, so suddenly, so irrevocably? I'll keep writing to you. I'll write now, even as my heart breaks, because this letter might be my last.

Oh, my dearest, my love, my angel!

Thank you for Reading

You've Just Read a Piece of the Greatest Library Ever Rebuilt

Thank you for reading.

This book is one of thousands we're restoring, reimagining, and translating as part of the **Modern Library of Alexandria** — a global movement to preserve and share humanity's most important ideas.

What was once lost to fire and time is now rising again — not just as memory, but as living, breathing knowledge, freely accessible to all.

What You Can Do Next:

- **Keep Reading.**

  Discover more legendary works — in beautiful print, audiobook, or digital form — at LibraryofAlexandria.com.

- **Build Your Own Library.**

  Every title is available as a paperback, hardcover, or collectible boxset — at true printing cost. Craft a personal library worthy of display.

- **Spread the Light.**

  Share this book. Tell others about the movement. Help us translate every timeless work into every language, so no reader is ever left behind.

By finishing this book, you've already taken part in something extraordinary.

Join us at LibraryofAlexandria.com

Together, we're rebuilding the greatest library the world has ever known.

With appreciation,
The Modern Library of Alexandria Team

Visit:

www.libraryofalexandria.com

Or scan the code below:

www.ingramcontent.com/pod-product-compliance
Lightning Source LLC
Chambersburg PA
CBHW011536260326
41914CB00007B/1172